WO...
101 GR...

Vol. 2

WORLD-FAMOUS
101 GREAT LIVES
Vol. 2

Ajay Kumar Kothari
Vishwa Mithra Sharma

PUSTAK MAHAL®
DELHI • BANGALORE • MUMBAI • PATNA • HYDERABAD

Publishers
Pustak Mahal®, Delhi

J-3/16, Daryaganj, New Delhi-110002
☎ 23276539, 23272783, 23272784 • *Fax:* 011-23260518
E-mail: info@pustakmahal.com • *Website:* www.pustakmahal.com

Sales Centres
10-B, Netaji Subhash Marg, Daryaganj, New Delhi-110002
☎ 23268292, 23268293, 23279900 • *Fax:* 011-23280567
E-mail: rapidexdelhi@indiatimes.com

Branch Offices
Bangalore: ☎ 22234025
E-mail: pmblr@sancharnet.in • pustak@sancharnet.in
Mumbai: ☎ 22010941
E-mail: rapidex@bom5.vsnl.net.in
Patna: ☎ 3094193 • *Telefax:* 0612-2302719
E-mail: rapidexptn@rediffmail.com
Hyderabad: *Telefax:* 040-24737290
E-mail: pustakmahalhyd@yahoo.co.in

© **Pustak Mahal, Delhi**

ISBN 81-223-0530-X

17th Edition : December 2005

The Copyright of this book, as well as all matter contained herein (including illustrations) rests with the Publishers. No person shall copy the name of the book, its title design, matter and illustrations in any form and in any language, totally or partially or in any distorted form. Anybody doing so shall face legal action and will be responsible for damages.

Printed at : United Colour Offset Press, Delhi

Preface

The World-Famous 101 Great Lives, part-II is one & the important volumes of our *'World Famous Series'*. It is being read to the extent that it has inspired our readers with an intrinsic desire to collect every volume of the series.

Keeping in view of the demands of our readers, we have now also carried out an extensive revision of the "Great Lives" series, by updating the facts and figures in the entries wherever necessary. While doing this, another factor was taken into account to make balance among Statesmen, Leaders, Philosophers, Scientists, Spiritual heads, Sportsmen, Musicians etc., with their carrier which succeeded one way or other in imposing the impact of their qualities over the people.

This revised fascinating edition (part-II) also looks at the lives of 101 successful men and women in their respective fields. It covers the pen-sketches of the persons like Saint Gyaneswar and Chaitanya, Social reformers like Nana Saheb Karve and Kabir, Revolutionaries like Savarkar and Ras Behari Bose, Statesmen like Disraeli and Bismarck, Scientists like Madam Curie and Swaminathan, Artists and Scholars like Birju Maharaj, Ala-Uddin Khan, Venkatesh Iyyengar, Bankim Chandra Chatterjee, and Amrita Pritam, Heads of States like De-Gaulle and Kamal Pasha, Sportspersons like Martina Navratilova and P. K. Bannerjee and many others.

In fact, these mini-biographies present the traits of 101 famous personalities in a nutshell.

We hope our readers will find this revised edition both interesting and useful.

—Publishers

CONTENTS

1. Saint Gyaneshwar 9
2. Euclid 10
3. Marcus Tulius Cicero 11
4. Pythagorus 12
5. Shankaracharya 13
6. Marcus Junius Brutus 14
7. Alfred The Great 15
8. Harsha Vardhan 16
9. Charlemagne 17
10. Babar 18
11. Aurangzeb 19
12. Shivaji Bhosle 20
13. Jyotiba Phule 21
14. Edmund Halley 22
15. Meghnad Saha 23
16. James Cook 24
17. David Livingstone 25
18. Thakur Kanwar Singh 26
19. Eamon De Valera 27
20. Adam Smith 28
21. Albert Schwitzer 29
22. Thyagaraja 30
23. Bankim C. Chatterjee 31
24. Ghanshyam Das Birla 32
25. Sir Shri Ram 33
26. Hans Christian Anderson 34
27. Sarojini Naidu 35
28. Tantya Tope 36
29. Jatindra N. Mukherjee 37
30. Prince Ottovon Bismarck 38
31. Dadabhai Naoroji 39
32. Nana Saheb 40
33. Shachindra N. Sanyal 41
34. Swami Dayanand Saraswati . 42
35. Swami Shradhananda 43
36. Alexander Graham Bell 44
37. Marie Curie 45
38. Jamshedji Tata 46
39. Benjamin Disraeli 47
40. Sarah Bernhardt 48
41. Ala-Uddin Khan 49
42. Ferozeshah Mehta 50
43. S. N. Bannerjee 51
44. Vasudev Balvant Phadke 52
45. Madan Lal Dhingra 53
46. Anne Besant 54
47. Vinayak D. Savarkar 55
48. Anna Saheb Karve 56
49. Mohammad Ali Jinnah 57
50. M. Visvesarayya 58
51. Ernest Rutherford 59
52. Kabir 60

53. Mahavir Prasad Dwivedi 61	79. Acharya Narendra Dev 87
54. Madan Mohan Malviya 62	80. T.S. Eliot 88
55. G.K. Gokhale 63	81. Khudi Ram Bose 89
56. Mahaprabhu Chaitanya 64	82. Ras Behari Bose 90
57. Swami Ram Tirth 65	83. Chandra Shekhar Azad 91
58. Sri Aurobindo 66	84. Ram Prasad Bismil 92
59. Bertrand Russell 67	85. Udham Singh 93
60. Gama Pehalwan 68	86. Govind Ballabh Pant 94
61. Mustapha Kamal Pasha 69	87. Rafi Ahmed Kidwai 95
62. Mohammad Ali 70	88. Abul Kalam Azad 96
63. Martina Navratilova 71	89. Dr. Zakir Hussain 97
64. Subramanya Bharati 72	90. General De-Gaulle 98
65. Franz Kafka 73	91. C. Rajagopalachari 99
66. M. Venkatesh Iyyengar 74	92. Ramakrishna Paramahansa . 100
67. Dr. S. Radhakrishanan 75	93. V. Shantaram 101
68. Clement Richard Attlee 76	94. Enricho Fermi 102
69. Dwight Eisenhower 77	95. Dr M. S. Swaminathan 103
70. Archibald P Wavell 78	96. Guru Teg Bahadur 104
71. George VI 79	97. Satyajit Ray 105
72. Mihir Sen 80	98. Birju Maharaj 106
73. P .K. Bannerjee 81	99. Amrita Pritam 107
74. David Ben-Gurian 82	100. Joseph Priestly 108
75. Sir James Chadwick 83	101. Amrita Shergill 109
76. Srinivas Ramanujan 84	
77. Shanti S. Bhatnagar 85	
78. Acharya J.B. Kripalani 86	

Saint Gyaneshwar

India : A Great Saint

Born : AD 1275   Died : AD 1296

Child prodigy Saint Gyaneshwar was a great scholar like his father. He was deeply interested in the study of scriptures and in religious practices. His extraordinary brilliance caught the eye of everybody. He tried to remove the social disparities by educating people through his experiences and anecdotes of life. He came to Newa in 1288. In 1289, he composed *Gyaneshwari* which holds pride of place in Indian scriptures, philosophical treatises and also in Marathi literature. He knew many languages, and so words from as many as 56 languages can be found in *Gyaneshwari*. He mastered the *Gita* when only 15 and set out on a pilgrimage with Saint Namdev. During his travel, he preached the essence of the *Gita*, emphasising on its aspects of knowledge, devotion and yoga, and composed *Amritanubhava*.

Born to a socially ostracized father Vithal Pant and mother Rukmini, Saint Gyaneshwar's childhood name was Gyandev. Both his parents were scholarly. He moved with his parents to Trimbakeshwar when only a child. He lost his parents at an early age. Orphaned and poor, Gyandev and his siblings had to depend on alms for their living. His preachings, however, brought him fame and extended his influence in the area. His pilgrimage took him to Alandi in 1296 where he attained *Samadhi*, while living.

A sizeable section of Indian society is still influenced by Saint Gyaneshwar's teachings. He is still alive in his *Gyaneshwari*. He is remembered with great reverence and devotion.

Euclid

Greece : Father of Geometry

Born : 350 BC **Died : 300 BC**

Euclid was a great mathematician of ancient Greece. Many a scholar and philosopher from Greece used to go to Egypt during those days. Euclid too established a school in Egypt. Though having scholarly inclination towards music, arts and optics, he was deeply interested in mathematics. He gave geometry a separate identity. Euclid had to face a lot of derision because his works, innovative as they were, were frowned upon by the suspecting public. He spent his entire life in research and in inventing new methods known as *Elements*. In *Elements*, Euclid summarized all the mathematical knowledge of contemporary ancient Greece into 13 blocks; those on geometry were taken as final authoritative works, of the subject for well over a millennium and still form the basis for many geometry text-books. In fact, most of the geometrical theorems that one has to learn at school were propounded by this Greek mathematician.

Euclid was born in Greece, of a shopkeeper father. Even in childhood, he used to be engrossed in points and lines. He was considered to be abnormal, which remained the cause of his unhappiness throughout his life. The then society neglected Euclid's great achievements and did not give him his due place, but time proved his findings to be true and established his authority in the field. Apart from *Elements,* he wrote some other works also, of which only a few are available today. Euclid enjoys pride of a place in the field of mathematics. His other ascribed works include *Phaenomena* and *Optics*.

□□

Marcus Tulius Cicero

Rome : *Diplomat and Orator*

Born : 106 BC   **Died : 43 BC**

Born in an ordinary family, Cicero rose to be one of the most powerful orators of Rome. He took up the legal profession after completing his education but could not get much recognition in it. It was his power of oration that rocketed him to popularity and fame and secured for him a high place in the administration of Roman Senate.

As a counsel, Cicero became indispensable to the administration. He was trained in the art of oration by Appollonius Molo at "Rhodes" Island where Molo had a school. Initially, Cicero appeared to be fired by revolutionary zeal but he was an inveterate imperialist. He helped the Government in crushing a revolt. This brought him into limelight. Soon, he became a close friend of Caesar. He was, like Caesar, much interested in literature and poetry. But he could not be of any help to Caesar in his re-construction projects. Cicero's tactic approval of Caesar's murder and his defence of the Republic known as First and Second Phillipes — a series of 14 great speeches made by him. In these speeches, he supported Octavian and severely denounced Antony. However, in autumn of C. 43, Antony and Octavian came to terms and Cicero was killed while trying to escape to the East.

Cicero was an effective orator, writer and statesman. As a statesman, he attempted unsuccessfully to carry out the moderate policy. His influence on the future of literature was immense. His prose was recorded as models of Latin prose, and his philosophical essays are full of common sense and practical sympathies. His informal letters to his two wives — both of whom he divorced — and to his beloved daughter Tullia, who died while still a young girl show the human side of a public figure like him.

Pythagorus

Greece : Ancient Philosopher

Born : 582 BC **Died : 507 BC**

Pythagorus was a Philosopher and Mathematician of ancient Greece.

In the study of geometry the "Pythagorus Theorem" is still the basic concept of geometrical studies on triangles. His philosophical ideas came to be known as "Pythagorian", and are concerned with the brotherhood of philosophers. He and his followers believed in the power of figures. For example, figure two stands for a line, three for surface, four for density, six for soul, seven for health and light, and eight symbolises love.

Pythagorus also claimed that metal wires can produce sound when stretched. He also demonstrated that tightening or slackening a piece of wire between two clamps varies the musical note it produces when it is plucked, and by doing so at regular intervals, a harmonic scale is produced. He accepted the theory of atom and believed in rebirth.

Pythagorus was born in the sixth century B.C. in Samos, an island of Greece. He was a moralist since his childhood. He settled in Crotona near Italy when he was 50. His teachings were new for his time and were opposed by the people. Many a time his meetings were disturbed because of his unconventional ideas. The Pythagorian methods gained ground only after his death, and his name became immortal in the field.

In scientific world, his theories on geometry, mathematics, astronomy, etc. were gratefully acknowledged. The famous astronomer Copernicus, for instance, described Pythagorus as a fore-runner of the suggestions put forwarded by him that earth and other planets rotate in orbit around the sun.

❏❏

Shankaracharya

India : Reviver of Vedic Culture

Born : AD 788   Died : AD 820

Shankaracharya's attempts to culturally unite the country in his short life span are unprecedented and unmatched to this day. He undertook the task of reforming and reviving religion at a time when the Indian society was deeply entrenched in many ills, conservative ideas and religious fanaticism. Shankaracharya travelled throughout the country and infused a fresh life in the dying Hindu religion. He expounded his theory of *Advaita* (monism). He was not only a great thinker but also a great organiser. Wherever he went, he compelled the great scholars of the day to concede defeat by sheer force of his scholastic arguments. To have forced the great Pandit Madan Mishra to bow before him was in itself a great achievement. By this, he tried to make these Pandits accept his philosophy of Vedic religion.

He is called *Jagatguru* because of his contribution towards spreading of vedic culture, and for establishing many centres for the same purpose in all corners of the country. At a very young age, he composed many religious books like *Brahmasutra, Manish Panchakam, Geeta Bhashya, Vivek-Chudamani, Prabodh-Sudhakar, Samvedanta-Sidhanta Sangraha*. In all these, he has explained the basis of his belief. These later became the tradition.

Shankaracharya was born in a Namboodiri Brahmin family at Kaladi in Kerala. At 18, he has studied and mastered *Vedas, Puranas* and *Geeta*. Shankaracharya brought about a new awakening in the Hindu society and has thus immortalised himself. He purged Hinduism of many evil cults and practices. He built the four sacred *mathas* in the four corners of India, Sringeri (Karnataka), Dwaraka (Gujarat), Puri (Orissa), and Badrinath (Uttaranchal).

Marcus Junius Brutus

Rome : *Caesar's Murderer*

Born : 85 BC   Died : 43 BC

Marcus Junius Brutus was brave Roman warrior. At the beginning, he remained as a supporter of Pompey — the great Roman general and statesman. During Roman civil war (49 B.C.), Brutus joined hands with Pompey against Caesar. After the defeat of Pompey, Brutus was pardoned by Caesar and was made a high-ranking official in his cabinet.

Nevertheless, Brutus plotted Caesar's assassination to restore the "Purity of the Republic" as he expressed to his countrymen.

In fact, Brutus was son of Cervelia, who was Caesar's keep. Though he was Caesar's illegitimate child, Caesar loved him much and tried in every way to help him rise in life. It is ironic, that though Brutus also loved Caesar, he did not compromise with his policies.

As Julius Caesar was attacked by the conspirators, Brutus plunged knife in his chest. At first, Caesar tried to defend himself, but when he saw that his very trusted man is the attacker, he gave up, exclaimed "You too Brutus!" and died. According to Shakespeare, Brutus defended his action to Mark Antony saying: "I weep for Caesar because I loved him, and I honour him because he was brave; but he was overambitious, and so I killed him". He married Procia, the daughter of Cato the Younger and so it was little wonder that while he felt great affection for Caesar, he nonetheless disapproved of all that the great man stood for.

Brutus was tactfully dragged into conspiracy to kill Caesar by some of the senators, but these people did not gain from this treachery. Soon after the murder, Brutus died of wounds sustained by his own sword after his defeat in the war.

Alfred The Great

England : Great Emperor

Born : AD 849 Died : AD 900

Though there have been about 60 odd Kings and Emperors in England, nobody, except Alfred, has achieved greatness and that is why he is known as Alfred, the Great.

In the early days, pirates from Denmark and Sweden used to attack England. Alfred fought them and though initially he suffered defeats, he ultimately defeated them at 'Slaughter Ford' and even pardoned them on accepting Christianity. He, in fact, halted the Danish invasions, making his Kingdom of Wessex—the nucleus of united England. Already a noted general he came to the throne in the middle of a Danish invasion which he had to buy off despite spirited resistance. By his tactful wisdom, he consolidated his army and navy and subsequently won a conclusive victory at Edington (878). He occupied London in 886 and was recognized as overlord of all England. Thus, he brought about peace and forged a new England.

Apart from being a shrewd Diplomat, Alfred was also a brave warrior, a scholar, a writer, an inventor and a law-maker. It was a great achievement for him to have not only defeated the pirates but also made them live peacefully in England, and contribute towards her progress.

Alfred worked towards spreading education and literature throughout England. He got ancient Latin books translated into English, himself doing a lot of translation. He wrote history of the period between Julius Caesar's attack on England and his own time. He also invented Candle Watch. He tried to regulate the English law, which to this day, is known as Alfred's Law.

Many of Alfred's descendants proved almost as able as he was.

Harsha Vardhan

India : Emperor

Born : AD 590   Died : AD 657

Harsha Vardhan ascended the throne in AD 606 when only 16, and the same year he started a new era popularly known as *Harsha Samvat*. He conquered the entire Northern region and annexed it to his kingdom to establish a strong empire. As an Emperor, he was well-loved by his public for his generosity, justice and love of the arts. He showed religious tolerance towards all religion, though he himself propagated Buddhism. His contribution in expanding Buddhism cannot be underestimated. He was a benevolent ruler and patron of Buddhism. Huen Tsang, the Chinese traveller, visited India during his reign.

Harsha Vardhan patronised art and literature. Banbhatt of *Kadambari* fame was his court-writer. Harsha Vardhan himself was a writer. He is known for his works *Naganand, Ratnavali* and *Priya Darshika*. Harsha was the last Hindu Emperor of India. He ruled over the entire 'Aryavart'. He had a commanding personality. As a ruler, he displayed kind-heartedness towards his subjects.

Harsha Vardhan was the son of Prabhakar Vardhan. He had a sister called Rajyashree. At the age of 16, he ascended the throne after the sad demise of his father but very soon he set out on his campaigns and emerged victorious on every front. He ruled for 40 years. During his reign, it was his practice to hold a conference of Buddhist monks every year.

Harsha Vardhan holds a place in history as a generous and brave emperor. He is remembered with reverence as one of the strong and able rulers of India. He extended his hegemony from Gujarat to Assam by war, but kept his empire decentralized and diligently oversaw local administration.

Charlemagne

Rome : *First Roman Emperor*

Born : AD 742   Died : AD 814

Charlemagne was born in Frank tribe. His father, Pepin, was the king of the Northern province. Charlemagne ascended the throne on the death of his father in AD 771. He had a gigantic personality with well disposed nature. He was a brave and good warrior. Charlemagne is remembered for re-establishing German Empire and for his attempts at reorganising Europe. For years, he expanded his empire by waging wars and conquered almost the entire Western Europe, including large parts of Italy. By AD 800, he was lording over Central and Western Europe. He used to fight in the name of God and converted most of Europe to Christianity. In response to an appeal by Pope Adrian-I, he waged a successful campaign against enemies in 773-74. Bavaria was annexed in 788 and Saxons and Avars were Christianised. The Pope Leo-III crowned him as 'Emperor of Holy Rome'.

At that time, Spain was under Muslim rule. In Baghdad, Haroon-Al-Rashid was the Khalifa (ruler). Charlemagne attacked Spain and conquered a large portion of it. While Haroon-Al-Rashid signed a treaty with him offering him gifts to ward off war. Thus, Islam could not reach Europe.

Charlemagne started studies at an advanced age. He learned to read but could not write. He had many scholars in his court. From his court he not only controlled an efficient administrative system, but also fostered the cultural renaissance, which spread through much of present-day France, Germany, Austria, Switzerland, Holland and Belgium. He gave education a new dimension by spreading network of schools and colleges. Charlemagne's rule can be said to have been shining moment in the millennium of turbulence that gripped Europe after the fall of Roman Empire.

Babar

India : Founder of Moghul Empire

Born : AD 1483   **Died : AD 1530**

The word "Babar", by which name the first Moghul Emperor in India is known, means a "lion". Babar's real name was Jahiruddin Mohammad. He was a descendant of the Mongol dynasty of Taimur Lung and Chengiz Khan, famous in history for their tales of cruelty as well as bravery. But Babar was a shade different from his illustrious ancestors. Whereas his predecessors reached Delhi, plundered the conquered land and escaped with the booty, leaving a wailing land to nurse its wounds, Babar chose to accept it as his own country and he stayed here to become a Hindustani. He never considered himself an alien. He vanquished Sultan Lodhi, captured the throne of Delhi, and established an empire after annexing the surrounding kingdoms to his territory. Babar made his reputation by conquest over Afgan rulers during 1522-29 thus providing territory that his grandson Akbar was to build into a great Empire. The foundation stone of Moghul rule in India was laid by Babar.

India was then divided into small kingdoms and principalities. Babar conquered a large area and brought the land under one rule. After a long time, here was a ruler who was trying to knit the territory into one body. By 1527, Babar was able to establish his supremacy over a large portion of India. It goes to his credit that instead of leaving India after looting it, he thought of being an integral part of it. He gave a stable administration to various provinces under him and brought them some semblance of law and order.

Babar had great aesthetic sense. He patronised art and some of the dormant and dead arts got a new lease of life. Babar also wrote his memoirs known as *Babar Nama*.

Aurangzeb

India : The Last Mughal Emperor

Born : AD 1618   Died : AD 1707

Aurangzeb, the 6th Mughal Emperor of India is remembered for many reasons. Whereas Babar was the founder of Mughal rule in India, Aurangzeb was the disintegrator. No doubt, Aurangzeb was a great Emperor and his period can be evaluated as a golden chapter in Mughal empire's history in terms of expansion, but his staunch pro-Muslim and anti-Hindu attitude brought about the downfall of the Mughal Empire. His despotic tendencies and fanaticism aroused much opposition which accelerated the process. He was a serious man by nature. Some years after he became emperor, he banned music at his court. He also dismissed all the poets, artists, historians that his father and grandfather had brought to the court.

Aurangzeb was the third son of Shahjahan. However, he removed his elder brothers from the scene, imprisoned his ailing father and ascended the throne. Shahjahan died in captivity and Aurangzeb became the Emperor of India.

Whereas on one hand Aurangzeb expanded the empire which was founded by his ancestors, Akbar *et al*, on the other hand he brought upon himself the wrath and opposition of the general public by his rigidity of ideas and his ill-treatment of his father and brothers. He imposed *jazia* (a tax) on Hindus. But, he himself had high morals. He used to meet his own expenses by sewing caps and writing verses from *Koran*. He fought many battles for expansion of his empire. He did strengthen it but his despotic rule resulted in its disintegration within 15-16 years after his death.

His latter years were spent in war with the princes of Rajputana and the Marathas. He had managed to undo all the good work that Akbar had done.

Shivaji Bhosle

India : Founder of Hindu-Maratha Regime

Born : AD 1627   Died : AD 1680

Shivaji is remembered in history with great veneration. Although a couple of foreign historians have tried to downgrade him, it is now proved beyond doubt that theirs' were partial and one-sided views meant to tarnish the image of a great ruler. No doubt, he dreamt of establishing a Hindu-Maratha empire, but he certainly was not against the Muslims. He was against the exploitation of Indian public by the then Muslim rulers and he tried to strike this fact into them. He had a large number of Muslim soldiers and officers in his army. He never disrespected Muslim women. Once when a Muslim woman was captured and brought to him after one of the campaigns, he sent her back to her camp with due honour and security.

Shivaji was born in April 1627 to Shahji Bhosle and Jijabai. His father wanted his son to be a 'noble' like himself in the court of the Muslim ruler of Bijapur, but this was not acceptable to Shivaji. At the age of 16, he collected the locals known as Mavale, organised them and attacked the surrounding forts which fell to him one by one. Very soon, the forts of Singhgad, Javali Konkan, Aurangabad, Surat were under him. In 1674, after conquering a large area, he established Maratha kingdom and was duly coronated. He was given the title *Chhatrapati*. He ruled according to Hindu system. In fact, Shivaji's guerilla war tactics were to prove fatal to the Moghuls and thereby he became a very special hero to the Hindus in the political climate of that time.

Shivaji's moral strength and his physical courage bore the deep influence of the teachings of Saint Tukaram, Samarth Ramdas and his mother Jijabai. He will always be remembered as one of the brave and intelligent rulers.

❏❏

Jyotiba Phule

India : *Great Reformer*

Born : 1827   **Died : 1889**

Jyotiba Phule was born at Kadgud in Satara (Maharashtra) to Govind Rao and Chimna Bai. As his father did farming of flowers, the family got the surname 'Phule'. Very intelligent since childhood, when Jyotiba entered his youth, he decided to participate in the struggle for freedom. He was against the ideals of then orthodox society of India. To him casteism and untouchability were the real enemy of people's unity. There was also a need for the upliftment of women through their proper education. For this purpose he opened a school for girls from all castes. Though he faced a lot of criticism and protest from the higher castes that did not affect his activities.

On November 16, 1852 Jyotiba was rewarded for his contribution for the upliftment of women through education. Jyotiba had arranged many marriages of widows too. He condemned unlawful abortion, child marriage, and polygamy. He opened schools and libraries for people of all the castes. In 1881, Jyotiba took active part in country wide protest by farmers. Later he established Satya Shodhak Samaj. This institution strongly condemned idol-worship, casteism, religious rituals and other social evils. He published a newspaper 'Deen-Bandhu' which was against the social evils. On September 24, 1887, he was awarded with the title 'Mahatma.' His famous books are *Gulamgiri, Eshara, Jatibhed Veveksar* and *Sarvajanik Satyadharma*.

Edmund Halley

England : Astronomer

Born : AD 1656   Died : AD 1742

Edmund Halley was a British Astronomer. Although astronomy was well-advanced by the 17th century and much progress had been done in spotting various planets, satellites, stars and ascertaining their movements and speed, astronomers were still puzzled by the comets appearing and disappearing suddenly. It was Halley who solved this riddle for them. The comet he first spotted and studied in 1682 came to be known as Halley's comet. He studied 24 comets. He also helped Newton in his research though he himself was much ahead of Newton in this field. He persuaded his friend Newton, to publish the *Principia*, which he also financed.

Halley was the first to find out and declare that comet (Halley's comet) would be seen after every 75 years which established that comet is also a rotating heavenly body like other stars. Halley also studied these comets that appear after a shorter gap, the shortest being three years and a half.

Halley had predicted the appearance of comet (Halley's comet) in 1986. It was found to have an elongated nucleus—15 km with a dark crust of dust, through which jets of gas shoot at high speed to produce its glowing head and tail. It will reappear in 2061.

His study of comets was extensive and intensive. He had established that comets revolve round the sun. Halley was Professor of Astronomy at Oxford University. The science of astronomy will always remain indebted to Edmund Halley for his inventive ventures in the study of comets.

Meghnad Saha

India : Famous Physicist

Born : AD 1894   Died : AD 1956

Many a scientist in India have gone unhonoured despite having done lot of work, whose importance is no less than that of actual invention or research. Albert Einstein, the originator of Quantum Theory, had published Saha's work in the German language. It is not the question of only translation, it was a matter of understanding the theory also.

Meghnad Saha was born in Saroyatali village in Dacca (now in Bangladesh) on 6 October 1894. His father owned a small shop in the village and wanted his son to study for few years and then look after the shop, but Meghnad had aptitude for studies. When he came to Calcutta for doing his M.Sc. he came into contact with eminent scientists like Jagadish Chandra Bose and Dr. Prafulla Chandra Ray. This brought Meghnad a new interest in science. He also got D.Sc. in astrophysics.

Dr Saha worked with many international scientists and also researched in the field of Astrophysics. He invented an instrument to measure the weight and pressure of solar rays. He produced the famous equation which he called "equation of the reaction — isobar for ionization" what later became known as Saha's "Thermo–Ionization Equation."

Dr Saha did not just sit and work in his laboratory. He was also aware of country's problem. In 1913, Pt Nehru appointed him Director of Indian Science Association. Saha was the leading spirit in organizing the scientific societies like the National Academy of Science (1930), Indian Institute of Science (1935), and the Indian Association for the Cultivation of Science (1944). The lasting memorial to him is, the Saha Institute of Nuclear Physics founded in 1943. He prepared the original plan for Damodar Valley project. He was also a member of Lok Sabha. He was interested in welfare of the nation apart from his involvement in scientific studies. On 16 February 1956, Saha collapsed while on way to Parliament and died.

James Cook

England : *Sailor and Discoverer*

Born : AD 1728   Died : AD 1779

It is an established fact of history that the Western world has made a significant contribution in discovering the new world. James Cook is known as a discoverer who set out on the sea to find new places. He was the first to discover river Lawrence of Canada. He also tried to study the way to Venus during one of his voyages in the Pacific Ocean. He is accredited for having surveyed the inner-most part of Canada as also for discovering Australia and its southern parts. In his later discoveries, he got the assistance of the British government. Cook made enormous addition to geographical knowledge and was responsible for Britain's acquisition of the Australian territories and his accounts of discoveries were classics. In fact, Australia and its southern countries were talked about, but no one had ever ventured there, nor anybody knew, for that matter, whether that land was a reality. James Cook undertook hazardous voyages and discovered the continent of Australia.

James Cook, however, discovered the coastal areas and found them fit for the British to settle there. But, unfortunately, the government did not take him seriously and sent only criminals there. Later, to prove his point, Cook himself settled there. The secret of James Cook's success was his skill as a sailor and his inborn leadership qualities. He was the first person to explore all the myriad land within, and on the rim of the world's largest ocean.

Cook was born at Marton in Yorkshire but he spent his life on board his ship, always on the move, in search of new lands. One of his sterling qualities was his ability to win the confidence of the native tribals and to work with them in unison. It is, therefore, ironic that he should be killed by the tribals. He was clubbed to death from behind on 14 Feb, 1779, while trying to recover a stolen boat from the islanders. He was then buried at sea.

David Livingstone

Scotland : *Explorer of Africa*

Born : AD 1813   **Died : AD 1873**

For many years, the continent of Africa remained unexplored and hence unknown. The main reason was the inaccessibility to its interior region due to dense forests, wild-life, savage tribals, deserts and barren solid hills. Many people tried to explore the land but could not survive the dangers. David Livingstone is among those brave few who not only explored part of Africa but also lived among the tribals bringing them near to social milieu. While others explored with the idea of expanding their respective empires, Livingstone did so to explore its vast and mysterious hinterland, rivers and lakes. He was primarily a religious man and a medical practitioner who tried to help mankind with it.

Livingstone was born in Scotland and was educated to become a doctor and a priest. His exploration started at the beginning of the year 1849. He reached Lake Ngami in 1849, followed the Zambezi to its mouth and saw the Victoria falls in 1855. He explored an unknown river in Western Luanda. However, he was reduced to a skeleton during several years of travelling. By this time, he had become famous and when he returned to England for convalescing, entire London, alongwith Queen Victoria turned to welcome him. After a few days, he returned to Africa.

He discovered the origin of the River Nile in 1866. He again suffered many discomforts. He became too sick and could not even walk. He lost contact with rest of the world that grew anxious to know his whereabouts. Ultimately it was Stanley, the American journalist, who found him after many efforts, but Livingstone had died in a tribal village in Zambia in 1873. His body was brought to London and buried in Westminster with full honour. He was the first European to explore many parts of Central and East Africa.

Thakur Kanwar Singh

India : Freedom Fighter

Born : AD 1782   Died : AD 1858

Thakur Kanwar Singh had the rare distinction of leading his forces as a General during the 1857 first war of independence, when he was 75. In fact, he had already reached ripe old age when he started taking part in political activities but with his zeal and quickness he had become model for youth. The revolt in Danapur, Bihar started with his inspiration. He organised the national rebels, attacked Aara and conquered it.

British efforts to recapture Aara were thwarted by Thakur Kanwar Singh's brave defiance. The British received a massive set-back when the Indian forces captured a large portion of Bihar including Jagdishpur and Azamgarh. When a British major attacked his kingdom of Jagdishpur, Kanwar Singh repulsed the attackers.

It would not be an exaggeration to state that the then Bihar had no other freedom fighter of the calibre of Kanwar Singh. After a couple of days, the English forces attacked Jagdishpur once again. During the siege, when the English forces were shelling and bombarding Jagdishpur, Kanwar Singh was wounded but that did not deter him. He just amputated his wounded right arm and threw it in the Ganga. This rare example of bravery was instrumental in his gaining a victory over the British once again.

Kanwar Singh ascended the throne of Jagdishpur after the death of his father. The title 'Raja' was conferred on him. Although he had all the qualities of a brave soldier since his youth, they remained dormant till he came into contact with Nana Saheb Peshwa. Once his zeal to fight for a cause was awakened, there was no looking back, nor could his advanced age be an obstacle. Thakur Kanwar Singh is remembered with great reverence among the freedom fighters of Bihar. He was the one who worked hard to make the freedom struggle a success.

Eamon De Valera

Ireland : Freedom Fighter

Born : AD 1882 **Died : AD 1975**

Eamon De Valera was a great revolutionary and freedom fighter. He was jailed for taking part in Easter-Revolution against Great Britain in 1916. He was sentenced to death which was later changed to life imprisonment. He was released from prison under an amnesty only after one year. He then became Chairman of Sinn Fein, the Irish National Party. He was re-arrested in 1918. On his release, he became a member of 'Dale' the Irish Parliament. On assuming power in 1932, he took many drastic steps and tried to break relations with England.

In 1937, he announced new legislation proclaiming it as 'Democratic Irish Free State'. He remained Prime Minister for 16 years from 1932 onwards. He was later elected Prime Minister for two more terms. Then he became President and remained so for 14 years. Throughout the World War II, he maintained strict neutrality. He contributed to the political freedom of Ireland as did Arthur Griffith and others.

De Valera was born in New York, the United States of America. He was the son of an Irish mother and Spanish father. He came to Ireland when he was two. He was a teacher of Mathematics after completing his studies, but he had to give up the job so as to fully participate in Ireland's freedom struggle. He was an able and forceful orator. He lived upto 93.

De Valera was a great patriot. He repeatedly paid for his views by imprisonment, and was regarded by both sides of the House with respect. Though England has retained one portion of Ireland, the credit to liberate the other half goes to De Valera. He constantly opposed the British sovereignty. He is remembered by the Irish people with great reverence and pride.

❏❏

Adam Smith

Scotland : Philosopher and Economist

Born : AD 1723   Died : AD 1790

In 1776, a book entitled *The Wealth of Nations* was published by a Philosopher and Economist which rendered great help to scholars and diplomats in their works in economics. This great work dealt elaborately with production and wealth and its exchange between nations. The author was Adam Smith, an Economist from Scotland.

Adam Smith was born in Kirkaldy, Scotland. After his education at Glasgow and Oxford Universities respectively, he worked as a Professor of moral Philosophy at Glasgow University. His *Theory of moral sentiments* was published in 1759. In 1766, he started his work on *The Wealth of Nations* which took him 10 years to complete. He believed in time-factor for making wealth. He drew his conclusion that political interference hinders the free-flow of trade and commerce. For him, money was a means to commerce not wealth in itself. For him, competition in trade and commerce without outside interference was healthy for growth. Smith advocated the free working of individual enterprise rather than the protectionism of mercantile system.

Smith was in favour of increasing the production of England. But, in the ensuing century, big landlords and feudal lords posed many obstacles in industrial development. Smith's later works came under scathing research and critical appraisal but his *Wealth of Nations* remains a classic in the field of economics. It was a searching analysis of division of labour, money, prices, wages and means of distribution. It had marked influence in political circle throughout the Western World. This work reveals its author's personality.

Albert Schwitzer

France : Religionist, Philosopher & Musician

Born : AD 1875   Died : AD 1965

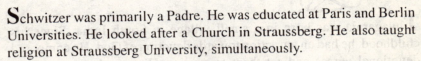

Schwitzer was primarily a Padre. He was educated at Paris and Berlin Universities. He looked after a Church in Straussberg. He also taught religion at Straussberg University, simultaneously.

In 1905, he gave up priesthood and started work in the field of Medicine. After being successful at home, he went to Africa to serve the African people in French colonies of Africa. He founded a hospital at a place called Lumbarne in 1913, giving organ recitals to support his work there. He arranged for the staff, medicines and the equipment from his own money and bore the entire cost of running the hospital himself. He devoted his life to the hospital he founded there.

Schwitzer had learned to play organ during his student days. He was one of the finest organ players in the world.

He visited Europe on a couple of occasions where he was given a rousing welcome. He was awarded Nobel Prize in 1952 for his notable contribution for teaching of *Reverence for Life* — dedicated for the cause of humanity. His many writings include *The Quest of the Historical Jesus* (1906).

He was a combination of a Religionist, a Philosopher, a Musician and above all a humanitarian all rolled into one. This amazingly saintly man died at the age of 90.

Thyagaraja

India : Karnatic Music

Born : AD 1767   Died : AD 1847

Thyagaraja was born in a small village in South India. Since his childhood, he had an attraction towards devotion of God. He composed devotional verses and set them to music. His popularity spread to the kings of the South as a great devotional poet and musician. The kings of Tanjavur and Travancore invited him to their courts but Thyagaraja did not wish to be a court musician. He was of the view that art cannot be weighed in money, nor can it be compensated by it. He politely declined these offers and chose to remain a commoner devoted to his art.

What distinguishes Thyagaraja in the field of poetry is his special sound-effect which revolutionised Karnatic music. He composed 700 verses and set them to music in 500 different *ragas*. Eighteenth and Nineteenth centuries are significant in the annals of Indian music because of him.

It is obvious from saint Thyagaraja's devotion to music that he was fully dedicated to his art. He was, indeed, an ancient ascetic in commune with the Divine Being. He was a devotee of Lord Rama. What he achieved in the field of music was not achieved by his predecessors of the fame of Tansen, Baiju Bawra and others who are known for their devotion to music. Tansen and Baiju Bawra are remembered for their contribution to music, likewise Thyagaraja will always be remembered for his valuable contribution to Karnatic music.

Known as "Sangeet-Guru" Thyagaraja is one of those precious gems of Indian music who set aside the lure of the court for the devotion of the muses.

❏❏

Bankim C. Chatterjee

India : Composer of National Song

Born : AD 1838   Died : AD 1894

The man to rouse the nation through 'Vande Mataram', Bankim Chandra Chatterjee; was a Deputy Collector when only twenty. He studied law and got the opportunity to become a Magistrate. From an early age, he was inclined towards literature. Gradually, he became a writer. In 1882, he wrote *Anandmath*. Besides, he also wrote novels *Krishna Charitra*, *Durgesh Nandini*, *Chandhrani*, *Visha Briksha*, *Kapal Kundal*a.

In his famous satirical book *Kamala Kanter Daftar*, he highlighted the social evils that prevailed in the society pertaining to injustice to the poor and he advocated remedial measures and degree of equality between have and have-nots in the society. This book is still considered as one of the most important treatises towards the concept of modern socialism.

Bankim Chandra Chatterjee was born on 27 June 1838, at Kantal-Para in West Bengal in a middle class intellectual family. His early education was completed at Midnapore. He was interested in sports and literature. He finished his studies from Presidency College, Calcutta, in 1856. He is considered to be a leading litterateur of Bengali literature.

Bankim Chandra composed the immortal 'Vande Mataram', a song that is now India's National song. All his works bear unmistakable stamp of nationalism and Indian culture.

On the death of his first wife, Bankim Chandra married second time. He died in 1894 at the age of 56.

Ghanshyam Das Birla

India : Industrialist and Nationalist

Born : AD 1894   Died : AD 1983

Ghanshyam Das Birla was a great architect of India's industrial growth. He started his career in Calcutta at the beginning of this century. He set up many industries. He entered the field of business during the days of the First World War, and established himself after the war years. First, he established a cotton mill in Sabzi Mandi, Delhi followed by Keshoram Cotton Mills and Birla Jute Mills around 1920. The Keshoram Mills was set up with the efforts of Andrew Yule. In 1919, with an investment of 50 lacs, the Birla Brothers Limited was formed and thereafter a mill was set up in Gwalior.

Mr Birla realized that political freedom from British rule was imperative for the industrial growth of India. In 1920, he came into contact with Gandhiji. In the decade of the 30's he set up sugar and paper mills. From 1943 to 1946, with stock exchange gaining ground, Birla Brothers ventured into the areas of cars, cotton, machinery and man-made fabrics. United Commercial Bank was set-up during this period. Prior to this, he had established Ruby, Asiatic Insurance Co and Inland Air Service.

After independence, the Birlas expanded their business and started production in many fields. Near Mirzapur, he, in collaboration with Caesar, an American friend, set up an Aluminium Plant Hindalco in record time. He bought the Century Mill from Sir Chunnilal V. Mehta, the cousin of Sir Purshottam Das Thakur Das. He also bought tea estates and started cement and fertilizer factories. In his birth place Pilani and at many other places he started many educational institutions. To his credit go many temples, planetariums and hospitals. In 1983, he died while in London. During the decades of 70's and 80's, Birla Brothers were among the topmost Industrial Houses of India. G.D. Birla award for Scientific Research has been established to encourage scientists for their contribution in the various fields of Scientific Research. ❏❏

Sir Shri Ram

India : Famous Industrialist

Born : AD 1883   Died : AD 1963

Sir Shri Ram started his career as an assistant secretary in the Delhi Cloth & General Mills, on a salary of rupees one hundred per month. By the time he died, he was one of the few noted industrialists of the country. He got the job in Delhi Cloth Mills only because his father Madan Mohan was also working there. Delhi Cloth Mills was at that time owned by the Gurwala family, the famous money-lender. Gurwala was a money-lender to the Nawab of Avadh and the Mughals in 1857. The family ran in ruins during the Bank Crises of 1913. At that time, even a prominent Bank like "People's Bank" closed down. The Delhi Cloth Mills also passed through a great crisis in 1917. However, it heaved a sigh of relief, when it got orders to manufacture tents for the British Army during First World War.

It is to the credit of Sir Shri Ram that he brought this Cloth Mill into the forefront of North Indian Mills. Sir Shri Ram was an able administrator. He had great knowledge of raw materials and cotton which was required for his mill. His idol was Tata. He engaged retired Civil Servants like Dr Dharamveer in the management of mill. Dr Dharamveer had occupied prominent governmental posts when in service.

In 1930, he established a sugar mill in Daurala, U.P. Today many diversified concerns of Delhi Cloth Mills are spread over various places in India, prominent among them being Bengal Potteries, Jai Engineering Works, Usha Sewing Machines, Shri Ram Fertilizers, etc. It was diligent, untiring hardwork, iron-will-power and great ambition that enabled a man, who himself earned rupees hundred a month to find employment for thousands of people. He has set an example for many of his fellow countrymen.

❏❏

Hans Christian Anderson

Denmark : *Author of Fairy Tales*

Born : AD 1805   Died : AD 1875

Hans Christian Anderson, the world-renowned author of *Fairy Tales* was born in Denmark of a poor cobbler. Could one imagine then that this child from slums would grow to be a world-famous writer of fairy-tales one day and a friend of the king of Denmark? Children all over the world read and enjoy his tales.

Anderson's personal life was not much different from his "Ugly-Duckling", a tale depicting the sad story of an ugly and neglected chick who turned to be a swan.

As a child, Anderson was lean, thin and dirty. He could not go to school for his parents had no money. He decided to be a singer. He set out for Copenhagen, the Capital of Denmark and tried to attract audience in the streets. But, unfortunately, his raucous voice and out of tune songs failed to attract the public. So, he tried his hand at acting and dancing with music but failed to move the people. While he was engaged in these gimmicks, an acquaintance of King Frederick VI spotted him. Moved by his plight, he pleaded with the King to make some arrangement for his education which the King did.

Anderson started writing for children when he grew up. In 1828, he wrote a successful satire, full of fun and laughter entitled *A Journey on Foot*. In 1835, his novel *The Improvisatore* brought him popularity. The king gave him financial assistance for travel across Europe. During his travels, he met many famous people but that did not vouchsafe fame. He earned great name and fame for his tales that transport us to fairy realm of dreams. Some of his famous works are *Onali-E-Fidlere, Poets' Bazar, Fairy Tales, Wonder Stories, Picture Books Without Picture, The Emperor's New Clothes,* and *The Snow Queen*. His other works include *Romances* and an *Autobiography*. Though in love twice, he could not get married. In fact, he died while an ascetic.

Sarojini Naidu

India : *The Nightingale of India*

Born : AD 1879   Died : AD 1949

Mrs Sarojini Naidu holds pride of place among women-freedom-fighters of India. She played significant roles in each and every movement arranged by Gandhiji and was always in the lead with men. She is also known as the nightingale of India, because apart from being actively engaged in national politics, she made a significant contribution to poetry. As a child, she wrote beautiful verses which impressed her British mentors also.

Gandhiji respected her. She represented him in various foreign countries. In 1919, she went to England. From 1922 to 1926, she was in South Africa to work for Indians there. Later, she went to America. She was the first woman President of the Indian National Congress in 1925 at the Kanpur session.

Sarojini was born in February 1879 in the Chattopadhyaya family of Hyderabad. She was educated at Cambridge, England and was later married to Naidu, a South Indian, as per her desire.

After independence, as a recognition of her services in the national, social and literary fields, she was made first woman Governor of Uttar Pradesh. She had also participated in the Round Table Conference of 1931 in England. *Feather of the Dawn*, *Golden Threshold*, *Bird of Time*, *The Song of India*, *The Broken Wing* are some of her well-known collection of poems.

Mrs Naidu's daughter Padmaja Naidu had also been on the social and political scene of India.

Tantya Tope

India : Hero of 1857 Revolt

Born : AD 1814   Died : AD 1859

The credit for making the first war of Independence a memorable event goes largely to Tantya Tope. A man with commanding personality, Tantya Tope had courage, agility, ability to take quick decisions, zeal, foresight and fortitude. He was of immense help to Laxmi Bai and Nana Saheb. He was the Commander-in-Chief of the rebel army of Shivrajpur. The victory of Indian forces at Kanpur was mainly due to his able leadership.

After capturing Kalpi, Tantya turned into the main fort of the rebels. He not only won many victories but also confused the British general by his guerilla tactics. While the British energy was entirely directed to search and capture Tantya Tope, he was busy organising the forces and engaging the British in minor skirmishes and ambush. His name was then synonymous with bravery and fortitude. Not that it was easy for him. For days together he would be wandering in jungles, facing unimaginable difficulties and hardships but still would hoodwink the enemy. However, he was unaware of a treacherer in his ranks and was deceived into being captured by the British on 7 April 1859. During his trial, he admitted boldly to his deeds saying everything he did was for the sake of his country and that he had no regrets. The first war of Independence ended with his death.

Tantya Tope was the only child of Pandurang and his wife Rukmabai. He was born in Yevla (Maharashtra) but brought up in Bithoor where Nana Saheb Peshwa resided. He loved Nana and dedicated his life for him. Tantya's real name was Ram Chander Rao. Tantya was involved with the rebellion since the Kanpur revolt and his life remained linked to the war of Independence right from its beginning to his own end on 18 April 1859. He was like the blazing sun of the rebellion rising with the first day of Kanpur revolt and setting when the patriots were crushed one by one.

Jatindra N. Mukherjee

India : Great Revolutionary

Born : AD 1879   Died : AD 1915

Jatindra Nath Mukherjee was known for brave deeds right from his childhood. He is among the forefront revolutionaries. He was born on 8th December 1879 at Nadia in Bengal. He passed his entrance examination in 1898 but in 1900, he gave up studies for the cause of revolution. 'Anandmath' inspired him to join the revolutionaries. He was jailed in 1910. He went underground to organise the revolutionaries. He played an important role in the Howrah conspiracy case. He pioneered the 'armed revolution' by reviving the revolutionary group 'Yugantardal'. Under his leadership, revolutionaries tried to capture Fort William at Calcutta, but failed. Kalighat was his centre of operations. He was popularly referred to as "Tiger Jatin". The British felt very much troubled by his activities and the British police had an uneasy time dealing with him. He was constantly locked in fierce encounters with them and did not give in during his lifetime. He attained Martyrdom on 9 December 1915 during an encounter with the police at Balasore where German arms were expected to arrive. A secret document prepared by James Chambell Ker, a British official regarding Jatindra Nath reads as follows. "Jatin's gang carried out in August 1914, the very successful coup which placed them possession of 50 Mauser Pistols and 46,000 rounds of ammunition belonging to Messrs Roddah & Co. of Calcutta."

Jatindra Nath is an example of bravery and nationalism for the youth of the country. He will always be remembered with reverence.

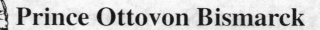

Prince Ottovon Bismarck

Germany : *German Statesman*

Born : AD 1815   **Died : AD 1898**

Bismarck's mission in life was to unite the small Prussian states into a single nation. Germany was divided into smaller states and a portion of it was called Prussia, which formed an important part. Bismarck had a towering personality and he nursed an ambition to play an important role in the German polity, right from his younger days.

His efforts saw him as a leader and foreign minister of Prussian council of ministers in 1862. Next year, he attacked Denmark to display his power. In 1866, he attacked Austria on a trifle matter. He won this battle also as he did against Denmark. Bismarck achieved many things through hardwork and a show of strength. He first organised and united the Northern states, and did likewise to Southern states and formed a unified Germany and was made its first Chancellor.

In those days, Germany had Chancellor as well as Emperor. Chancellor was head of the government while Emperor was head of the State. Bismarck did his best for the upliftment of Germany. When Kaiser ascended to the throne, he made Bismarck a 'Prince'. Bismarck was considered to be a very important person throughout Europe.

Though Bismarck fought many small battles, his main aim was to unite Germany. He himself did not favour wars but during his lifetime militarism grew in Germany which laid foundations for the two World Wars in future. He tried to secure his works by a triple alliance with Austria and Italy (1881), but ran into difficulties at home with Roman Catholic Church and the Socialist movement, and was ultimately dismissed by William II in 1890. Bismarck retired to his castle near Hamburg to write his memoirs in which he predicted World War I (1914-1918) and Germany's defeat.

Dadabhai Naoroji

India : Founder Member of INC

Born : AD 1825   Died : AD 1917

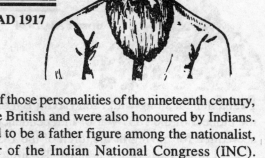

Dadabhai Naoroji is one of those personalities of the nineteenth century, who were respected by the British and were also honoured by Indians. In fact, he was considered to be a father figure among the nationalist, being a founder-member of the Indian National Congress (INC). Dadabhai not only worked towards attaining Independence but also inspired many educated people to join hands with him.

Dadabhai Naoroji was born on 4 September 1825 in a Parsi family. In 1845, he did his B.A. and ten years later went to London. There, he assisted Bhikhaji Cama, a leading businessman, in his business. He organised the Indians living in London and formed the Indian Society. After sometime he was chosen to be a member of the British Parliament. He was perhaps the first or second Indian to have the honour of becoming member of the British Parliament. He was known as "The Grand Old Man of India."

When Dadabhai joined Congress, it was basically a society of Government servants and its main function was to apprise the British government of the people's problems. Dadabhai was extremely popular and was elected as its President in 1896 and 1906. Dadabhai was not satisfied with merely petitioning the complaints to the government. He sought Independence. He was summoned to the court for his activities and asked for sitting in the court.

Dadabhai Naoroji is among those leaders who did not overlook the importance of keeping in touch with the British while demanding Independence. He is also acclaimed as the "Father of Indian Politics and Economics".

Nana Saheb

India : *A Great Freedom Fighter*

Born : AD 1824   Died : AD Uncertain date

Nana Saheb, along with Rani Laxmi Bai of Jhansi, is remembered as the pioneer of the 1857 war of Independence. In fact, Nana Saheb was accredited for having lit the torch of the 1857 revolt and spreading its light to other parts of the country. He himself took up the sword and spread the message of freedom through personal example of courage.

The background for the war of Independence was prepared by Nana Saheb with the help and co-operation of Rango Bapuji and Azimulla. He contacted various royal houses, chief among them being Bahadurshah and Wajid Ali Shah at the outset of the revolt. He set out ostensibly on a pilgrimage but in reality these journeys were meant to muster support for a revolt against the British regime. On May 27, 1857 he captured Kanpur and on 28 June 1857, at Bithoor, he was enthroned ceremoniously as a ruler and a victor. But, soon after the ceremony he got engaged in a fight with Havlock, the British general in Kanpur. He struggled hard for success. The facts regarding Nana Saheb's death are not known for certain.

Nana Saheb was born in June 1824 at Venu in Maharashtra. His father was Madhav Narayan Bhatt and mother Ganga Bai. He was adopted by Peshwa Bajirao as his son in 1827. He was given a sound moral education and trained as a soldier. Tantya Tope and Laxmi Bai were his childhood friends. Nana Saheb was brave and talented. In 1851, when he succeeded Baji Rao Peshwa, the British denied him his pension which embittered him and the British became his sworn enemy. His ability to prepare for the revolt speaks of his bravery. Many British writers have praised him for his irrepressible courage, fortitude and generosity. Nana Saheb was instrumental in bringing Hindu-Muslim together to fight under one banner.

□□

Shachindra N. Sanyal

India : Great Revolutionary

Born : AD 1895   Died : AD 1945

Shachindra Nath Sanyal was born in Benaras where he completed his education. He started participating in revolutionary activities from his student days itself.

Shachindra Nath jumped in the independence-struggle fray in 1908 when he formed Young Men's Association. The same year he came into contact with Ras Behari Bose and gave Hindustan Republican Association a revolutionary outlook. He also came into contact with the members of *Gadar* Party.

He was jailed in Benaras in 1915. The British sentenced him to life imprisonment and he was sent to Andaman. However, he was released but was rearrested in 1925 during Kakori conspiracy. His health deteriorated in Gorakhpur jail, but he did not give up and underwent imprisonment many more times. Ultimately, he died in Gorakhpur jail in 1945, at the age of 50.

Throughout his life, Sanyal showed great penchant for revolutionary literature. He wrote *Jailed Life* which is an autobiography. He will always be remembered for his dedication and involvement in the cause of the nation.

❏❏

Swami Dayanand Saraswati

India : *Founder of Arya Samaj*

Born : AD 1824   Died : AD 1883

Swami Dayanand is remembered with reverence and affection among the social reformers of the nineteenth century. He raised his voice against idol worship. That was a time when religious hypocrisy was rife, social evils like child marriage was an accepted practice, widows were ill-treated. It was Swami Dayanand who showed remarkable courage in decrying these practices and instituting reforms. At the Kumbh fair of 1876 in Haridwar, he spoke openly against social evils and kept his views frankly in favour of widow remarriage. He established the glory of *Vedas* and founded a progressive and reformist society, which he named Arya Samaj. He was a great Sanskrit scholar and admonished his followers to go back to the *Vedas*. His works *Satyarath Prakash*, *Rigved Bhumika* etc. are well known. He also wrote a treatise on the *Vedas*.

Swamiji was born at Marvi in Gujarat. His name was Mool Shankar. Young Mool Shankar was much above the mundane. He ran away from home when his father forced him for marriage. He reached Mathura and studied *Vedas* and other scriptures under a *guru*, Swami Virjanand. As his tuition fees, he pledged to his *guru* to serve and spread the knowledge of *Vedas* and the truth all his life. He fulfilled his promise.

For Swami Dayanand, foreign rule was never tolerable. He was a patriot and a social reformer. Many of his principles were accepted and adopted by Gandhiji. It is believed that Swamiji participated in the 1857 war of independence. His works have been pioneering in the social field and will always be the torchbearer for others on this path. He was an incarnation of kindness and forgiveness for he forgave a man who gave him poison.

❏❏

Swami Shradhananda

India : Originator of Gurukul System

Born : AD 1859 Died : AD 1926

Swami Shradhananda left an indelible mark of his works on the spiritual progress of the country. He founded the institution Gurukul Kangri with a view to spreading education. This helped in spreading female-education and also in improving the image of Hindi language. He edited *Saddharma Pracharak* in 1889, *Shraddha* in 1918, *Vijay* in 1919 and *Arjun* in 1924 and through these he spread the nationalist feelings among masses. He was President of 1913 Hindi Sahitya Sammelan. He is known as a social reformer and spiritual patriot.

Born as Munni Ram, he spent his youth in voluptuous and luxurious living. He was an atheist but an encounter with Swami Dayanand changed him into an ascetic and a patriot. He was considered to be the heart of Delhi and was a symbol of Hindu-Muslim unity. He was the first Hindu to have roused the people of Delhi to patriotism from the ramparts of Jama Masjid. He was the one who bared his chest to the gun-wielding soldiers of the Viceroy in the Chandni Chowk procession.

Shradhananda's works will never be forgotten. He gave India a new awakening in spiritual, national and moral obligations.

Alexander Graham Bell

Scotland : An Inventor

Born : AD 1847   Died : AD 1922

"My God, it speaks" uttered the Emperor of Brazil and the receiver of the Telephone slipped from his hand and banged aground. At the other end Alexander Graham Bell was still on line.

This incident goes back to 1876 when at an exhibition in Philadelphia (USA), Alexander Graham Bell was giving a demonstration of his new invention. This strange instrument known as Telephone was to revolutionize human life in the years to come.

Bell was born at Edinborough, Scotland. He was a teacher and was dedicated to the noble cause of teaching the deaf and the dumb. Due to a severe illness, Bell was sent to Canada in 1870, where too he got engaged in helping the dumb-deaf to hear and speak. Thereafter, he shifted to the USA but continued with his work by opening a school for deaf and dumb.

In 1873, he became Professor of vocal physiology at the University of Boston. Bell was fond of scientific inventions and was ever engaged in making some machines in his spare time. While at Boston, he tried to communicate through metal wire. His companion in this work was Watson. One day while experimenting with his instrument, Bell spoke to Watson standing at a distance. Watson was taken by a pleasant surprise as he had heard Bell clearly through his instrument. The instrument was a success and Bell patented it.

Graham Bell had some sterling qualities of head and heart. Apart from being an artist, he was a kind human-being, ready to help the needy. He established an institution for the deaf and dumb children. He died in 1922 in Canada. The entire northern America paid him a tribute by hanging up their telephones for a while during his funeral. By giving us telephone, Bell has made our world a smaller place.

Marie Curie

France : Discovery of Radium

Born : AD 1867   Died : AD 1934

Marie Curie was born to the poor parents in Warsaw, the capital of Poland. She was Christened Mania. She wanted to go for higher studies but her parents were unable to do so because of poverty. However, due to insistence of friends and relatives, she went to France for higher studies where she completed her M.A.

That was a time when women were not considered equal to men and were relegated to backstage. It was believed that women were incapable of achieving anything in the field of arts and science. Ironically, Marie Curie is the only Nobel Laureate to have won the coveted prize twice, and Madam Curie was a woman!

She married Pierre Curie, while in Paris and became Marie Curie. Both husband and wife were interested in research in Physics and Chemistry. They started working on Radium. They did not have enough wherewithals to use a sophisticated laboratory. They used to experiment under a dilapidated roof, which often leaked during rains. Ultimately, their perseverance paid and they discovered Radium and its activity in 1903. Both husband and wife were awarded Nobel Prize in 1903. In 1911, Marie Curie was again awarded the Nobel Prize for research in Chemistry. She was appointed Professor of Physics at Paris University. The French Govt. also set up a centre for research called the Curie Institute of Radium, with Marie as the Head. Her published works include *Recherches Sur Les Substances Radioactives* (1904) and *Traite de Radioactive* (1910).

Pierre Curie died in 1906 in a road accident. Marie survived him but died of cancer in 1934. It is ironic, isn't it, that the inventor of Radium which is used in the prevention and cure of cancer should die of cancer!

Jamshedji Tata

India : *Pioneer of Indian Industry*

Born : AD 1839   Died : AD 1904

Jamshedji Tata is considered to be the path-finder of modern industrial builders. He is known as the grandfather of Indian industry for his acumen and enthusiasm. Nobody else could have thought of the new industries started by Jamshedji at that time when industrial awakening and revolution was yet to come to India.

Jamshedji's father Nasarvanji Tata used to trade in jute with China and Britain. He started export from India. Jamshedji started a cloth mill in Nagpur more than hundred years ago. At that time almost all the cloth used to come from Lancashire in England. What Jamshedji did was praiseworthy.

Jamshedji knew very well that an industrial revolution can only be brought in the country by setting up iron and steel industry. Although he did not live to see the industry he had in mind, he had done all preliminary work. In fact, he laid about the ground work for it. He had planned the entire steel city, now known as Jamshedpur, complete with streets, roads, schools, parks, playgrounds, temples, mosques, churches, etc. His dream was fulfilled by his sons, Sir Dorabji Tata and Sir Rattan Tata, when they started the Tata Iron & Steel Factory in 1907 just after three years of his death. Today, Tata Iron and Steel Company Ltd. has the largest assets of Rs. 4924.39 crore as estimated for the year ending 1994 — with a growth rate of about 20%.

Tata knew that science education was necessary for strengthening the roots of Indian industry. He established the Indian Institute of Science (IISc) at Bangalore. The hydro-electric project at Bombay is an example of his foresightedness. The Taj Hotel in Bombay was also built by Tata, which ranks as one of the best hotels in the world.

❏❏

Benjamin Disraeli

England : *British Statesman*

Born : AD 1804   Died : AD 1881

When a slim and young Jew British member of Parliament rose to make his first speech, he was jeered at by the members. The 32-year old MP sat down saying, "I will sit down today but the time will come when you will be listening to me attentively", and that time did come when later he was twice the British Prime Minister. Disraeli was an independent member of Parliament in his first year. Later, he joined the Conservative Party. He became Prime Minister for the first time in 1868, but the liberals won the next elections. However, in 1874 he again became the Prime Minister. He was the founder and chief inspiration of the modern Conservative Party.

Disraeli holds a prominent place in the British politics for many reasons. He passed a bill to stop the illegal strikes that had become daily occurrences. He passed the Merchant Shipping Act which stopped over-loading of ships. Besides, he adopted a successful foreign policy. When Russia planned to occupy certain parts of Turkey at the Berlin Congress, he sent a British armada to help Turkey. He sent troops to Afghanistan to prevent Soviet troops from entering India through Afghanistan.

One of his outstanding and bold acts was to acquire shares in Suez canal from the King of Egypt, without the approval of Parliament. The Parliament was not in session at that time but the Act was wholly in favour of England. England paid forty lakh pounds and got the right to use the canal which was a considerable shortcut route to India. His imaginative policies and foresight brought him great success and popularity. His Government was defeated in 1880, and a year later Disraeli died after writing his famous book *Endymion*. His other works include *Life of Lord George Bentinck* (1852) and *Lothair* (1870).

Sarah Bernhardt

France : *Famous Actress*

Born : AD 1844   Died : AD 1923

Many great actresses of the world have made history and Sarah Bernhardt was one of them. For 50 years, she dominated the field of acting. Although her first performance was remarkable for its high quality of acting, yet she kept on improving with every performance till the end. Her work never sagged.

Sarah was born in Paris. She was educated at the famous school of drama of France. She was, in a strange way, so different from her other colleagues that for many days she was not given a chance to come on the stage. But in 1870, when she got a chance, she displayed extraordinary talent. She acted different characters successfully of which "Joan of Arc" and "Elizabeth-First" were outstanding roles. She studied and acted many men characters of which "Hamlet" was quite famous.

Sarah had to have one of her foot amputated after an accident in 1914, but that did not deter her from performances. Even today many actresses try to copy her style. Sarah Bernhardt is respected by all the stage-lovers of the world.

Ala-Uddin Khan

India : Classical Music Maestro

Born : AD 1869   Died : AD 1972

Ustad Alla-Uddin Khan holds an important place among the classical music maestros of India. He had an inclination towards music since his childhood. He was taught by Nanu Gopal, Nandlal and Vazir Khan. The Raja of Mehar, a connoisseur of music, made him his *guru*. On 19 October 1958, he was awarded 'Padma Bhushan' and in 1971, 'Padma Vibhushan'. He joined hands with Uday Shankar, the famous dancer, in staging shows abroad which earned him fame. He dedicated his life to music and music only. All India Music Festival is organised every year to commemorate his contribution to music.

Alla-Uddin came of the farmer stock of Shipur (Tripura). He had an unquenchable urge for music since his childhood which forced him to leave his home when eight. Facing all odds, he continued learning music and with the passage of time his talent shone. For a while, he worked for a drama company. He died on 6 September 1972. His wife was Madina Begam.

Ustad Alla-Uddin Khan remained engrossed in music till last, although he was a centurion. His contribution in this field will ever be remembered. His life is a symbol of the fact that one can reach the peak if one works with unabated efforts.

◻◻

Ferozeshah Mehta

India : Liberal Freedom Fighter

Born : AD 1845   Died : AD 1915

Ferozeshah Mehta was born in a Parsi family of Bombay, Maharashtra on August 4, 1845. After graduating in 1864, he went to England to study law. He returned home in 1868 after getting his Bar-at Law in 1867, but soon after joined the freedom struggle instead of continuing with Law.

A representative of the liberals, Sir Ferozeshah was for achieving freedom through constitutional means. He was foremost among those who formed the Indian National Congress and continued working to tidy it. He chaired the 6th session of the Congress in 1890. Sir Ferozeshah wanted radical changes in higher education. He started propagating his views through *The Bombay Chronicle*, started in 1913.

During those days, highly educated people tried to project their grievances through an organisation which later took the form of Congress. Even high-ranking British officers attended its sessions but later when Sir Ferozeshah became its President, the government barred him from attending the session because it was felt that the Congress was turning into a nationalist organisation and demanding independence.

Sir Ferozeshah Mehta continued his efforts for freedom through constitutional means. His contribution to our freedom struggle is immeasurable. He died on November 5, 1915.

❏❏

S. N. Bannerjee

India : Founder-member of INC

Born : AD 1848   Died : AD 1925

Surendra Nath Bannerjee is one of those national leaders who played a leading role in the establishment of the Indian National Congress. He held extremist views and was considered a militant till Lokmanya Tilak's arrival on the scene. In the beginning, he was assigned the task of liaison with the government. He was the Congress representative to highlight the difficulties, problems and views of the organisation to the British government through appeals, petitions and deputations. Although, he was honoured with knighthood and became 'Sir Surendra Nath', he could not toe the British line of thought. He felt he was being made a pawn by the British. He wanted much more for India than mere verbal assurances.

Surendra Nath was born in Bengal. He cleared his ICS examination when twenty-one. For a while, he worked as a professor of English before jumping into national politics. He chaired the 11th Congress session of 1895 and the Ahmedabad session of 1902.

Surendra Nath made his mark as a writer also. His autobiography *A Nation in the Making* is a masterpiece. Some of the great ideals mentioned in his book are (i) the creation of a strong body of public opinion in the country (ii) the promotion of friendly relation between Hindus and Muslims and (iii) the inclusion of the Indian masses in the great public movements of the day. He was one of the most influential leaders of Bengal of that time and was emulated and respected by the youth. "Ripon College" which is now named after him is a living example of his incessant and massive work in the field of education.

Vasudev Balvant Phadke

India : Firebrand Revolutionary

Born : AD 1845   Died : AD 1883

Vasudev Balvant Phadke was born in a Brahmin family of Ratnagiri (Maharashtra) on 4 November, 1845. Contact with nationalist leaders like Mahadev Govind Ranade and others influenced him in his early days to fight for the cause of freedom. But soon, he was attracted towards militancy. He was fired by revolutionary zeal and killed many a Britisher in guerilla activities.

Phadke is remembered with great respect among those who tried to respond to British tyranny and oppression with revolutionary fervour rather than with non-violence. In fact, he believed that non-violence was not the effective way to freedom. In 1879, he was tried and sentenced to imprisonment on the charge of anti-government activities. The inhuman treatment meted out to him in jail and the torture he was subjected to told upon him. Badly broken in physical health, Phadke died in jail on 17th February 1883.

Phadke holds a significant place in the annals of India's freedom struggle for his tactics of guerilla warfare. He collected young men with fervour for freedom and organised them so efficiently that the British government had to be always on the alert to fend for a surprise attack from any quarters—imaginable or unimaginable.

Phadke was an ideal revolutionary and a patriot of first water. He will always hold a high place in the annals of India's history.

Madan Lal Dhingra

India : *A Fearless Young Revolutionary*

Born : AD 1887   Died : AD 1909

Madan Lal Dhingra will always be recalled as one of those fearless young revolutionaries who jumped into the fight for freedom without ever looking back at life, family and parents. Madan Lal will remain immortal as a young rebel who wrecked vengeance on the English oppressors in their own country. He avenged their tyranny in India, and on Indian public by killing the guilty in their own land.

Dhingra was born in a well-to-do Khatri family of Punjab. After graduating from the Punjab University, he went to England for further studies. But, when he learnt of British oppression in India, he shot dead two officers.

Madan Lal Dhingra was only 22, young and full of happy dreams. But, he sacrificed a happy and secure future for his motherland. It was but a small sacrifice for a big cause. During his trial, he admitted that he had taken the extreme step for his motherland and added, "In the service of my country I have nothing but my blood," such words, such courage — Madan Lal Dhingra's name is immortal.

Although the propounders of non-violence downgraded the Indian revolutionaries, this does not, in any way, reduce the importance of their deeds for a noble cause. Can one ever question those sentiments because of which they sacrificed everything at the altar of their motherland?

This great revolutionary died in the same jail where Sardar Udham Singh was immortalised. Madan Lal Dhingra was a symbol of the youth of his time who were strongly opposed to the oppressive measures adopted by the British ruling India with an iron hand. It was an insult to them and their motherland which they could not tolerate.

❏❏

Anne Besant

India : The Founder of Home-Rule League

Born : AD 1847 Died : AD 1933

Among the successful women of the world, Anne Besant tops the list. She was so influenced by the Indian religion, philosophy and spirituality that she identified herself fully with India and became an inveterate Indian. Her contribution to India's freedom struggle was also remarkable. She founded the Home-Rule League with support and co-operation of Lokmanya Tilak. She revived the Theosophical Society. In the field of social work, education and journalism, her contribution cannot be over-estimated. In 1917, she was elected President of Indian National Congress. She also edited *New India*. She received a prestigious award for her work for scouts. India will always remember with relish, her works in the social, educational, spiritual and national fields.

Anne Besant was born in London to the Irish parents. In 1893, she left for India having been influenced by the Indian culture and civilization. In 1914, she participated actively in all political activities here and was in favour of granting India its freedom. She also studied Hinduism. She died at a ripe old age of 86.

Even today, India remembers with gratefulness Anne Besant's immeasurable work for freedom struggle, educational advancements and social reforms. She established Indian Boy Scouts Association. Many Indian leaders were impressed by her liberal ideas.

❑❑

Vinayak D. Savarkar

India : Brave Revolutionary

Born : AD 1883   Died : AD 1966

Vinayak Damodar Savarkar was a great patriot, a scholar, a poet and a writer all rolled into one. He started patriotic activities even in his student days. At the age of 16, he founded *Abhinav Bharat*. It would not be an exaggeration to call Savarkar a born revolutionary.

He was not awarded his B.A. degree, which he passed from Ferguson College, Pune, due to his revolutionary activities.

He was arrested and jailed for his nationalistic activities. When he was being brought to India from England to face trial, he jumped off the ship into the sea and swam into the French territory. It was an unprecedented and unparalleled act of bravery and for many such brave acts he is called *Veer* meaning brave.

Savarkar wrote many books, among them *The First War of Indian Independence* is a prominent one. Savarkar came into contact with many revolutionaries of the world during his sojourn in England. He himself was revolution personified. He also championed the cause of Indianness.

Savarkar suffered many hardships at the hands of British, but his courage and his devotion never flagged. His name has been immortalised in the annals of Indian history.

❏❏

Anna Saheb Karve

India : A Great Reformist

Born : AD 1858   Died : AD 1962

Anna Saheb Karve's life was as simple and clean as that of an ancient ascetic (Rishi-Muni). He was liberal in his views and sympathetic in his attitude. He was deeply moved by the troubles and tribulations of women-folk.

What Anna Saheb did for the upliftment of women in the last decade of the nineteenth century was beyond the imagination of the people. He created an awakening among women through his writings in *Kesari*. He was a staunch supporter of widow-remarriage. On March 11, 1893, he himself set an example before the society by taking a bold step of marrying a widow. He established an orphanage in Pune.

Anna Saheb realised the importance of education for women. He spared no efforts in starting Bharatiya Mahila Vidyapeeth, the first university for women. In 1921, he travelled to Europe and America, met famous people like Albert Einstein and formulated his opinions regarding work. In 1958, he was awarded 'Bharat Ratna' in recognition of his services in educational and social reforms.

Born on 18 April 1858 at Ratnagiri, Maharashtra, Dhondopant rose to be Dr D.K. Karve. In 1884, he graduated from a college in Bombay. In 1891, he lost his first wife and later remarried a widow in 1893. The couple dedicated their lives to social work and reforms. An old veteran of 104, Dr Karve died in 1962.

Mohammad Ali Jinnah

Pakistan : Qaid-e-Azam

Born : AD 1876   Died : AD 1948

Mohammad Ali Jinnah was the creator of Pakistan and was the Governor-General of Pakistan after partition of India in 1947.

Jinnah tried to steer his country out of chaos of partition trauma. Pakistan was faced with Hindu-Muslim riots, famine, refugees, and many other problems. However, Jinnah's astuteness was able to withstand it all.

Jinnah was a leading lawyer of his time. He joined the Congress and participated in the Independence struggle. However, he thought that Gandhiji was favouring Hindus at the cost of Muslims, a feeling which was fanned by the British. As a result, Jinnah formed Muslim League and demanded a separate state for the Muslims. His views on creation of a separate state of Pakistan were recognized by the Crips Mission of 1942 and at the 1946 conference in London, he insisted on the partition of British India into Indian and Muslim States. He became first Governor General of Pakistan after the transfer of Power in August 1947.

During the interim period, out of sheer frustration, the Muslims started killing Hindus in the Muslim dominated areas. Punjab and Bengal were ravaged by communal riots. Indian leaders saw partition as the only way out. Jinnah died soon after partition and was honoured with the title of 'Qaid-e-Azam' (man — number one).

M. Visvesarayya

India : Prominent Engineer

Born : AD 1862 **Died : AD 1962**

Mokshagundam was India's leading Engineer. He helped in building many dams and bridges in the country after independence. In fact, he is considered as one of the founders of modern India.

Soft-spoken, gentle and efficient, Visvesarayya can easily be termed the builder of modern India if one were to refer to the construction work he undertook. He worked towards the benefit of the country with complete devotion.

Visvesarayya also worked as a *Dewan* for the Nizam of Mysore and was the inspiration behind Mysore University. He can be credited with having given a modern look to many of our cities. His selfless devotion earned him knighthood (the title 'Sir') during the British raj. He was honoured with "Bharat Ratna" in the year 1955.

Dr Mokshagundam Visvesarayya was born on 15 September 1861 at Mudanhalli in Karnataka. His parents were poor. After completing his B.A. from Bangalore Central College, he joined Engineering and passed it in 1883 with high marks. He also travelled extensively in Europe. He showed his administrative ability in every field wherever he was posted. He was highly appreciative of the Japanese and their progress impressed him. He died in the year 1962 of old age.

Dr Visvesarayya has left an indelible mark on the nation. His birth anniversary is celebrated every year with great enthusiasm.

Ernest Rutherford

Britain : Scientist

Born : AD 1871   Died : AD 1937

Ernest Rutherford was born at Nelson in New Zealand in 1871. He was extremely brilliant — a child prodigy, indeed. He used to work on his father's farm when he was a student. He received a scholarship to study at Cambridge University, where he studied science.

By that time, research in the field of atomic activity had made tremendous progress. Marie Curie had discovered radium activity, but the reason for that activity was not yet known. It was left to Ernest Rutherford to dive into research in this area.

Rutherford published his findings in 1911 and these findings and the results threw much light on the structure of the atom. A new field was opened in Nuclear Physics. It was only after this that the atomic bomb could be made and atomic energy developed.

Rutherford did his research in the laboratory of the Cambridge University. Later, he became Professor of Physics at the McGill University in Canada. He was the Director of the Cavendish Laboratory, Cambridge during 1919-1937. The University had not seen anything like him before. He dominated nuclear research there for a generation and took a leading part in all the achievements. He gathered about him the most distinguished accumulation of younger brains ever to be assembled in a place of science. He was knighted by the British Government in 1914 but earlier in 1908, he was awarded Nobel Prize for Physics. In 1929, he became the first physicist to be created a Baron. Sir Ernest Rutherford holds a pride of place in the world of physics.

A pioneer of modern atomic science, his main researches were in the field of radioactivity and he was the first to recognize the nature of the atom.

Kabir

India : *A Nirgun Bhakti Poet*

Born : AD 1399   Died : AD 1518

Saint Kabir, a *Bhakti* poet gave a severe blow to the ostentatious and dead customs of Indian society. His poems are read and sung even today with great relish. He was not only a litterateur of the *Bhakti* period but was also a social reformer. He tried all his life to unite the Hindus and the Muslims and preached against useless religious practices which divide people instead of uniting them. He believed in a formless God *(Brahma)* and was strongly opposed to the divisive caste-system. He is considered to be the exponent of Hindu-Muslim unity. He showed the society a new way by dragging it out of its orthodox practices and bigotry. His works have been compiled in *Shakti, Sabad, Kamaini* and *Beejak*. His riddles are also well-known.

Kabir was born in a Hindu family but was brought up by a Muslim couple. His mother's name was Loi. When touched by the saintly Ramanand at Kashi Ghat, Kabir felt elevated. He accepted Ramanand as his *guru*. He was a weaver by profession. Although not much educated in terms of conventional educational system, he was a proponent of reformist ideas which were new for his time.

Kabir died in Maghar. His death raised a controversy regarding his last rites as to whether it should be according to Hindu practice or Muslim practice. It is said that when the shroud was lifted there were just a few flowers lying where the body lay.

❑❑

Mahavir Prasad Dwivedi

India : Hindi Poet

Born : AD 1864   Died : AD 1938

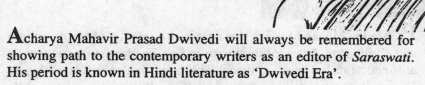

Acharya Mahavir Prasad Dwivedi will always be remembered for showing path to the contemporary writers as an editor of *Saraswati*. His period is known in Hindi literature as 'Dwivedi Era'.

Dwivedi joined government service initially. In 1903, he became editor of *Saraswati* and thereafter for 15 years he worked zealously for the cause of Hindi. He was a successful essayist. He wrote on many topics. He was a critic also.

Dwivedi contributed greatly towards the development of *Khadiboli*. His well-known works are: *Rasagya Ranjan*, *Sahitya Seekar*, *Sahitya Sandarbha*, *Adbhuta Alapa*, *Sanchayana*, *Dwivedi Kavya Mala* and *Meri Jeevan Gatha*.

Dwivedi was born in Daulatpur in Uttar Pradesh. He acquired knowledge of Hindi, English, Urdu, Bengali, Gujarati and Marathi. He kept his interest alive in literature even while working for the Railways. His wife was of great help to him. He died at 74 after enriching Hindi literature.

Dwivedi was an inspiration to many new writers. He is considered to be the leader of his time. He has left his stamp on literature which can never be blotted.

Madan Mohan Malviya

India : Propounder of Hindu Culture

Born : AD 1861   Died : AD 1946

Pt. Madan Mohan Malviya was a staunch supporter of Hindu culture and civilization. His contribution to India's freedom struggle, as well as to education has been significant. The establishment of Benaras Hindu University is the result of his untiring efforts. It is interesting that while collecting funds for the university, he approached even Maharajas, Rajas, rulers and landlords who did not subscribe to his views and yet, strangely, they all contributed open-heartedly and willingly for his cause. None dared refuse him, so appealing was his approach and so convincing were his reasons for a donation.

Madan Mohan Malviya belonged to a poor family. He was born on 25 December 1861. He was a bright student. After graduating in 1891, he joined law but later jumped into the arena of freedom struggle. It is ironic but true that he was loved by both Indian masses and British officers.

Mr Malviya was an Indian to the backbone. He subscribed to the Indian culture and kept his ideas intact all his life. He gained name and fame because of the work he did for social, ethical and educational upliftment. He is called *Mahamana* and is loved by all. For the poor, he had special feelings. Dressed in immaculate Khaddar *Pyjama-Kurta* and a head-gear, his image remains ever in the hearts of the people. Unfortunately he died in 1946—a year before India got independence.

□□

Gopal Krishna Gokhale

India : Gem of Maharashtra

Born : 1866   Died : 1915

He has been aptly called by Lokamanya Tilak, his lifelong rival, "The diamond of India, the gem of Maharashtra." Gokhale was born on May 9, 1886 at Kotluk in Ratnagiri district in the Kolhapur State of Bombay Presidency. He came of a poor Brahmin family. Later he graduated in 1884 from the Elphinstone college, Bombay. Gokhale's brother wanted him to go to England and compete for the ICS but, he chose the humbler profession of teaching. Later he came under the influence of Justice Ranade, and then under his expert guidance began the study of Indian Economics.

In 1900, he was elected as a member of the Bombay legislative council where he worked along with Sir Pherozeshah Mehta. In 1902, he was nominated to the Viceroy's Council, where his budget speeches were well known for financial criticism.

He was elected the president of the National Congress of Benaras in 1905. His presidential speech is considered as one of the best ever delivered on the congress platform. Gokhale was a champion of the interests of the Indians abroad. He supported their agitation in South Africa against the humiliating disabilities imposed upon them. This interest in the South African problem brought him into close contact with Gandhi. He supported Gandhi's passive resistance campaign.

He had played a significant role in India's freedom movement. For years he stood forth, in the eyes of both the Indian Government and the British Democracy as the most representative Indian. He never merely abused and criticized the Government when he dealt with the shortcomings as some of his contemporaries did. He was in a larger sense, a reconciler between the Western and Eastern culture. Gandhi had affirmed him as his political guru.

❑❑

Mahaprabhu Chaitanya

India : A Great Religious Reformer

Born : AD 1486   Died : AD 1533

Mahaprabhu Chaitanya was born in February 1486 at Nawadweep in Bengal. His parents were very religious-minded persons. Chaitanya's original name was Vishwambhar and he was nick-named 'Nimai'. He was also called "Gawranga Maha Prabhu". His parents did not want him to study much as they feared he might renounce the world.

Chaitanya got an opportunity to study Sanskrit and its grammar. This enabled his intellectual capacity to come to the forefront. He was married to Laxmi, daughter of a learned priest, but she died of snakebite and he married Vishnupriya. A great change came over him at twenty-two and he renounced the world. His life now took a complete turn.

Chaitanya completely immersed himself in the worship of Lord Krishna by singing *kirtan*. His singing group became part and parcel of Bengali life. He gave a new turn to the religious fervour in Bengal. His area of influence increased considerably because he was good to his detractors also.

He went to Puri where he attracted the masses to his philosophy. He went to south India in 1510 and then travelled western India.

He influenced people with his religious beliefs wherever he went. He went on pilgrimage again in 1513 and travelled the entire North India in 1515. Thereafter for the next 18 years he remained in Puri. He was a follower of Radha-Krishan and gave a new direction to the *Vaishnava* religion in Navadweep (Bengal), Puri (Orissa) and Brindavan (Uttar Pradesh). Throughout his life, he was immersed in religious activities, and will always be remembered for it.

Although he did not write extensively he exerted a profound influence on the subsequent development of Bengali and Oriya literature.

He died in 1533 A.D.

Swami Ram Tirth

India : A Vedantic Scholar

Born : AD 1873   Died : AD 1906

Swami Ram Tirth was born on 22 October 1873 at Murli, Gujaranwala (now in Pakistan). His father was Pandit Hiranand and he was extremely poor. Ram Tirth was initially named Tirth Ram. He studied Urdu, Persian and Sanskrit. He stood first in B.A. He declined to appear for the ICS examinations because of his inclination towards the spiritualism. In 1899, he got attracted towards the Himalaya and set out to travel there.

Swami Ram Tirth mesmerised Father Scott with his knowledge and was drawn towards spiritualism after finishing his education. He announced renunciation at a young age and became famous all over the world in 1901. He went to Japan in 1902 and enthralled the public there with his preachings. He lighted the lamp of Indian spiritualism in the United States of America also. He impressed thousands of people during his travels.

While on his way back to India from America, Swami Ram Tirth stayed in Egypt for few days. He preached in Persian in a Mosque there and attained great fame. He was greatly honoured there. Swami Ram Tirth also wrote many books. He also indulged in *Shairi*.

Throughout his life, Swami Ram Tirth emphasized on individual and national independence. He was a path finder for the youth. He attained *Samadhi* on the Dipawali day on 17 October 1906.

❏❏

Sri Aurobindo

India : *Revolutionary and Philosopher*

Born : AD 1872   Died : AD 1950

Aurobindo Ghose can be called a revolutionary-ascetic who propounded direct political action than moderate reformism but ended being an ascetic, spreading the message of divine peace and love. As a revolutionary, he is honoured in India for his nationalistic fervour but as a philosopher, the world admires him for his divine vision. Vehement though his activities were, they could not last long. After the 1907 sedition case there came a sudden change in his life. He sailed for Pondicherry in 1910, set up an *ashram* there and adopted the sedate life of a philosopher-thinker. He is called "Risi Aurobindo".

Sri Aurobindo tried to assimilate Indian and Western philosophical thoughts and find the paths of divine communion and spiritual realization. He believed in spiritual and cultural evolution of man along with attainment of worldly goals.

Sri Aurobindo was born in Calcutta. He was educated first at Darjeeling, then was sent to England. He passed his ICS but could not relish serving the British empire. He worked for some time with Sister Nivedita.

Maharshi Aurobindo stayed mainly at Pondicherry and was engrossed in meditation. The *ashram* was looked after by 'Ma', the mother. His *ashram* attracts visitors from all over the world. Even today the *ashram* is a centre of meditation and a seat of studies on Aurobindo.

He wrote many brilliant philosophical books among which *Life Divine* and *Essays on Gita* are considered the best among the lot.

Bertrand Russell

Great Britain : *Controversial Philosopher*

Born : AD 1872   Died : AD 1970

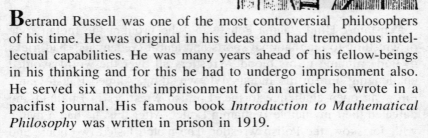

Bertrand Russell was one of the most controversial philosophers of his time. He was original in his ideas and had tremendous intellectual capabilities. He was many years ahead of his fellow-beings in his thinking and for this he had to undergo imprisonment also. He served six months imprisonment for an article he wrote in a pacifist journal. His famous book *Introduction to Mathematical Philosophy* was written in prison in 1919.

Bertrand Russell taught Mathematics at Cambridge after finishing his education. He criticized Great Britain for participating in the First World War and asked allies to stop the war. He was disqualified from the membership of Trinity College for his so called antinational utterances. He went to Russia after the war and was greatly impressed by the Marxist philosophy and became an ardent follower of it. He had to face severe criticism for his views which were very radical. He was also against the prevalent social and moral codes of Europe.

Despite his unorthodox behaviour, he wrote many brilliant treatises. Among his works *History of Western Philosophy*, *Human Knowledge: Its scope and limit* and *The Analysis of Matter* are well-known. In 1951, he wrote his famous book *New Hopes for a Changing World* which is still considered as the most important work on global social revolution. He was awarded 'Order of Merit' in 1949 and Nobel Prize in 1950. He was deadly against atom bomb and Vietnam war. He even staged a sit-in demonstration in front of 10, Downing Street, the official residence of British Prime Minister. The world plunged in mourning on the death of this incomparable philosopher.

Gama Pehalwan

India : World-Famous Wrestler

Born : AD 1880   Died : AD 1960

"Rustam-e-Hind" Gama Pehalwan, who brought the Indian style of wrestling to international sports and lent it credentials, had tricks of trade running in his blood. Wrestlers all over the world avoided challenging him in the Indian-style wrestling. Ahmed Baksh Gama threw an open challenge to the English wrestlers in England and defeated their invincible Benjamin Loller. After this, he had a match with Jeviskow, the Polish wrestler. The match lasted two hours and forty five minutes but Jeviskow could not be defeated. A re-match was fixed for the next day but Jeviskow turned tail and fled from England. In the ensuing year, Gama defeated Maurice Deriyaz and Ormond of international fame and achieved invincibility in the ring.

In 1910, a wrestling match was organised for the award of the title 'Rustam-e-Hind'. Gama defeated all the wrestlers and earned the title. In 1922, Jeviskow reached India for a match with Gama, who defeated him in just 42 seconds. Gama's last match was with J.C. Peterson whom he defeated in 45 seconds.

Gama wrestled for many years and always emerged victorious. However, one of his greatest quality was that he had not only a sense of self-respect but was very friendly in nature. Indian wrestling owes its popularity to Gama.

Ahmad Baksh Gama was born in Datiya (Madhya Pradesh) of Kashmiri parents. He was fond of wrestling since his childhood. By 20, he had defeated almost all the national-level wrestlers. For a couple of years, he was with Maharaja of Patiala. Later, he shifted to Lahore, where he remained after partition also. Unfortunately, later part of his life was full of want, poverty and misery. He died in Lahore on 22 May, 1960.

❏❏

Mustapha Kamal Pasha

Turkey : Builder of Modern Turkey

Born : AD 1881   Died : AD 1938

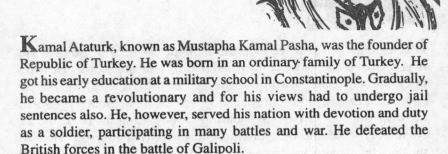

Kamal Ataturk, known as Mustapha Kamal Pasha, was the founder of Republic of Turkey. He was born in an ordinary family of Turkey. He got his early education at a military school in Constantinople. Gradually, he became a revolutionary and for his views had to undergo jail sentences also. He, however, served his nation with devotion and duty as a soldier, participating in many battles and war. He defeated the British forces in the battle of Galipoli.

Constantinople was earlier capital of Roman empire. They called it New Rome. Thereafter, everybody who ruled Turkey, including Ottoman, made Constantinople the center of international politics. Britain, France and Russia tried to advance towards Black Sea through it. At that time 'Young Turks' established the modern Turkey by finishing the Ottoman empire. Kamal Ataturk's name is prominent among these people. He made Ankara his new capital. Ataturk means "Father of Turks".

Kamal Ataturk assumed Presidency of Turkey. He abolished certain laws relating to religion and laid more emphasis on nationalist policies than religious ones.

He laid greater stress on education and social reforms and brought western education to Turkey. Today, Turkey is free from faddists. In Turkey, Western culture is growing side by side its ancient culture. It has a rare combination of new and old. The credit for it goes to Kamal Ataturk. He ruled as virtual dictator who introduced many positive social and administrative reforms which affected Turkish religion, justice, education, language and the status of women.

❏❏

Mohammad Ali

USA : World Boxing Champion

Born : AD 1942

Mohammad Ali is a well-known name in the field of Boxing. He is considered the most controversial Boxer in the world. He won international championship at the age of 18. At the 1960 Rome Olympics, he was a gold-medalist. It was on 25 February 1965 that he won the world title by beating Sonny Liston. Then on 22 November 1965, he beat boxing-giant Flyoyd Patterson. He had thrilling bouts with Joe Frazier only to be defeated. But Ali defeated Joe in a return match in 1974.

Mohammad Ali defeated George Foreman on 30 October 1974 and Leon Spinks on 15 September 1975. Thus he was world heavy weight champion during 1964-67 but he was stripped of the title for refusing military service. He considered himself the 'Great' for being the world champion. He interested himself in political affairs also and was often in the news for his various activities.

Mohammad Ali was born on 17 February 1942 in a Negro family. He was very strong from childhood. He was born as Cassius Clay, but later he embraced Islam to join the Black Muslim movement and changed his name to Mohammad Ali. Initially, though despised by people he has now achieved great popularity all over the world. He visited India with his wife Veronica. He has earned a lot of money in 61 bouts and is supposed to have won over 70 lakh dollars in the ring.

The film *The Greatest* is based on Mohammad Ali. In 1962 New York Times published his famous utterance which reads as under:

"I am not only greatest, I'm double greatest. Not only do I knock 'em out, I pick the round". He remains the greatest, even now.

❑❑

Martina Navratilova

USA : World Famous Tennis Player

Born : AD 1956

Anyone with a little interest in sports is bound to be familiar with the name Martina Navratilova. The name and fame she has earned in the Tennis World has no equal. She is rated at the third place in all-time Women Tennis Greats. She has lost on very few occasions.

Martina was born in Prague, in October 1956. She was a very enthusiastic player from her childhood. So, she started participating in various championships. She, however left Czechoslovakia and settled in the United States of America in 1975 due to certain personal reasons. She is now an American citizen. She has won a record nine titles of Wimbledon Tennis Championship for women (single) during 1978-79, 1982-87 and 1990. Her total of 45 Grand Slam event titles is second only to Margaret Court's record of 66. She also won women's double in 1978 and 1979. Of the twenty-five championships held in 1979, she won half of them. She also won US Open 4 times during 1983-87.

Age has not been a barrier to Martina, unlike other players. She won Grand-Slam in 1983-84. In 1990, she won six events in the Grand-Slam championships.

Martina is one of all-time greats of Tennis World. She had won over US$ 19 million in prize money upto 1994.

In 1994, she bade goodbye to tennis career.

❏❏

Subramanya Bharati

India : *National Poet*

Born : AD 1881   Died : AD 1921

Subramanya Bharati was a poet of modern Tamil. His compositions taste of patriotic fervour. The king of Ettimpur was so impressed by his writings that he conferred on him the title "Bharati" when Subramanya was just 11 years old, and also made him his court-poet, the poet laureate. In 1905, when Bengal was to be partitioned, Bharati expressed his anguish in his poems. He edited *India* and *Bal Bharati*. He was also active in politics and attended the Varanasi session of the Congress. His collection of poems *Swadesh Geet* was published in 1907. In 1918, he was imprisoned for writing inflammatory verses. In 1920, he edited *Swadesh Milan*.

Bharati was born on 11 September, 1881 at Tinebelli in Tamil Nadu. Nick-named "Subaiyya", he was a child prodigy who started writing when only 7. By 1908, as a student of class X, he was composing beautiful poetry. *Kopal Pattu* and *Panchali Sapatam* are his famous poems. He died on 11 September 1921.

Subramanya Bharati served the cause of the nation through his pen. The nation will always remember him for his fiery verses which instil zeal in the youth. These verses are dripped with his love for motherland. In Tamil Nadu he is almost a household name. He was a great patriot as well as a philosopher. His impact on Tamil literature is great.

Franz Kafka

Czechoslovakia : German Author

Born : AD 1883   Died : AD 1924

Kafka is considered a very interesting writer of modern Germany. He was unfortunate in not getting attention during his lifetime. He could get only a couple of stories published during his lifetime, while a large number of his works was later edited and published by his friend Marx Brand. His was a lonely and anguished existence. His mental state is clearly reflected in his writings which are full of alienation and desperation. His ideas influenced literature of later years. For Kafka, literature meant happiness derived out of terrible torture. He searched wholeness in fragments. His famous works are — *Judgement, Stoker, Penal Colony, Country Doctor, Hunger Artist, The Trial, Meditation.* The credit for bringing his works into limelight goes to his friend Marx Brand. The world today recognizes their depth and the existential strain in them. His work is marked by themes of oppression. The best known of his short stories is *The Metamorphosis* published in 1915, in which a man turns into a beetle. His work is marked by the themes of oppression.

Kafka was born on 3 July 1883 in Prague, Czechoslovakia, in a Jewish family. He had planned to study German language but by the time he entered Prague University, he developed interest in literature, so he completed his doctorate instead, and in 1908, he started working for an insurance company. Kafka remained a bachelor but he had some good women friends. His love-affairs with Dora, Felis and Hansy are well-known. He died when forty. But in life he saw agony only.

He was a Jew and was subjected to neglect and torture which told upon his mental peace. His literature speaks of the agonies of life and its harsh realities. Like Talmud, he reveals in his writings the futility of human existence and the absurdity of human situation.

❏❏

M. Venkatesh Iyyengar

India : Kannada's Great Novelist

Born : AD 1891   Died : AD 1986

Srinivas Iyyengar, Kannada's prolific novelist was popularly known as 'Maasti'. He is known as a revolutionary novelist. He was awarded the 'Gyanpeeth Award' in 1983 for his famous work *Chikkavir Rajendra*. He wrote nearly 120 books, which contain 18 plays, 30 novels, 46 biographies, 17 poems and 17 collection of stories. His first work *Kelpoo Sanna Katheguk*, a collection of stories was published in 1920.

'Maasti' who was known as the grandfather of Kannada literature, was born in a middle class family in Kolar district. His mother tongue was Tamil. However, he was beyond the confines of any language tangle and rose like meteor in the Indian literature. He contributed towards every aspect of literature. He was brilliant from an early age. He was selected for administrative services of the then Mysore state in 1914. He rose to become Chief Secretary in 1943 and then opted for voluntary retirement.

During his career 'Maasti' got experience in the various social and administrative field. He was familiar with both urban as well as rural way of life.

His writings depict all the characters from Royal persons to labourers, farmers, pious persons and even crooks. This was the result of his deep study of human character and its understanding.

'Maasti' never sought awards and decoratives, though throughout his life he was bestowed upon with such honours. His name ranks equal to that of Prem Chand and Sharat Chandra in the field of Indian literature. It was a great coincidence that he died on his birthday, 6 June 1986, when he completed 96 years.

❏❏

Dr. S. Radhakrishanan

India : Great Philosopher & Teacher

Born : 1888   Died : 1975

Dr. S. Radhakrishanan is known the world over as a great philosopher, a teacher, a speaker, a writer, a diplomat and a statesman. He was the second president of India after Dr. Rajendra Prasad.

Sarvepalli Radhakrishnan was born at Tirutani in Madras. In 1921, Radhakrishanan joined the University of Calcutta as King George V Professor of Mental and Moral philosophy. The Andhra University honoured him with the degree of D.Litt. In 1939, Pandit Madan Mohan Malaviya honoured him by making him the Vice-Chancellor of the Benaras Hindu University.

In 1949, the then Prime Minister Jawahar Lal Nehru sent him to the soviet Union as an ambassador. There he proved to be a very successful diplomat. He distinguished himself as the Vice-President of India (1952-62).

Radhakrishanan was elected the president of India in 1962. The Queen of Britain conferred on him honorary membership of the Order of Merit. In December 1964, Pope Paul VI made him "De Equastrine Ordine Militae Auratae," the Vatican's highest honour of a Head of State. In February 1975 he was awarded the Templeton Award. He was the first-non-Christian to get this award. He was also a brilliant author. Among his over 150 books, the more famous are his two volumes of *Indian Philosophy*, his editions of *Upanishads*, the *Bhagvatgita*, the *Brahmasutra*, *Dhammapada*, *The Hindu View of Life*, *The Reign of Religion*, *Religion and Society*, *The Philosophy of Tagore* and *Future of Civilisation*.

Radhakrishanan was a saint by personality; and humanity was his religion. He was conferred the Bharat Ratna in 1954.

Clement Richard Attlee

England : British Politician

Born : AD 1883   Died : AD 1967

Clement Attlee became the Prime Minister of England after the Second World War. Winston Churchill who had successfully led England and the allies to victory over Hitler was now rejected by the English people at the hustings. Labour Party swept to power and Attlee became the Prime Minister in July 1945. One of his memorable tasks was that he was instrumental in granting India its freedom.

Attlee was born in a well-to-do family but he always had great concern for the poor and the downtrodden. He is known for keeping harmony and cooperation among his cabinet colleagues. Not that there were no differences of opinion among his cabinet members, but Attlee, by his gentle nature and positive approach, always managed to keep them together and had control over them. Besides being sympathetic to the cause of India, and granting India freedom, he did many a constructive activity for his country too, like nationalization of some industries, and starting National Health Scheme.

Attlee's Labour party lost elections in 1951. He remained the opposition leader till 1955. He was awarded the Order of Merit and became a member of the House of Lords as Lord Clement Attlee.

India will always remember him for his kind and sympathetic attitude towards her and for granting her freedom. His pipe-smoking posture is as famous as Churchill's cigar-smoking image. His books include *"The Labour party and Perspective"* (1937) and *"As it Happened"* (1954) — an autobiography.

Dwight David Eisenhower

USA : General and President

Born : AD 1890   Died : AD 1969

General Dwight David Eisenhower was popularly known as "Ike" throughout the world. He was so popular at that time that 'I like Ike' was a common refrain in the United States of America.

Eisenhower was basically a soldier. He was the General in the army in 1942. However, he had no experience of a major battle. During the Second World War, he was appointed Commander-in-Chief of the US forces by President Roosevelt and in the 1944 campaign in France, he was Commander-in-Chief of the allied armies. It was his generalship and farsightedness that brought about Hitler's downfall and the allied victory.

He was elected President twice — in 1952 and 1956. In foreign affairs, he ended the Korean war (1950–1953) and established a network of military alliances around the world, but refused to commit military forces to civil war heating up in Vietnam. Eisenhower held office during a period of domestic and international tension, with growing civil rights movement at home and the cold war dominating international politics. He has been favourably assessed for maintaining stability in a time of crisis. The civil Rights legislation of 1957 and 1960 were among the most significant measures of his presidency.

Eisenhower travelled throughout the world during his tenure. He also visited India where Indian public gave him a rousing welcome. With his beaming smile, his kind, quiet, reassuring voice, he embodied the solid, reliable father-figure that so many of his countrymen longed for.

He retired at the age of 70—the oldest President to complete his term in the office.

Archibald P. Wavell

England : *British Field Marshal*

Born : AD 1883   Died : AD 1950

When Wavell was appointed as Viceroy of India in 1943, it was considered as a bold decision. Britain was involved in war with Japan and Germany and Indian struggle for independence was at its peak. The British had to contain both the home front as well as the war front. However, Wavell prepared such a groundwork that his successor Lord Mountbatten's task was made very easy.

Wavell is considered one of the important British generals of this country. It was ironic that he always had to face the most difficult situations throughout his career. Many a times he had to retreat inspite of careful planning. He was Commander-in-Chief of British forces in the Middle East from 1939 to 1941. He conducted the North African War against Italy in 1940-41 and achieved notable success there as well as in Ethiopia. Britain faced acute shortage of men and material at that time. He faced and suffered defeats on many occasions. Unfortunately, he very seldom had anything but tough commands to carry out, where there was no hope except skilful withdrawal. Wavell was sent to India as the Commander-in-Chief when the Japanese were launching a full scale attack on the country. And later, he succeeded Lord Linlithgow as Viceroy during 1943-47 in India.

A brave soldier, Wavell was also an intelligent and an emotional person. He loved English poetry and knew most of it by heart. He could recite these for hours. He was adept at doing translations from Latin and Greek to English. It was commonly said that a gentle hearted personality like him was rarely found in a soldier.

❏❏

George VI

***England** : British Monarch*

Born : AD 1895   Died : AD 1952

George VI was undoubtedly one of the most popular kings of England, where Royalty still exists despite being a democratic country.

Albert Frederick was the second son of King George V and Queen Mary. Albert ascended to the throne because his elder brother Edward VIII had to abdicate it as he wanted to marry a common woman and that too an American divorcee. Thus Albert Frederick became George VI. His special trait was that he was very shy but also very brave. In 1923, he married Lady Elizabeth Bowes-Lyon and their children are Elizabeth II and Princess Margaret.

King George VI remained in London during the Blitzkrieg by German planes in Second World War. He remained unperturbed even when a bomb fell on Buckingham Palace and damaged a portion thereof. He even went to the various parts of London to inspect the damage caused by bombing. He went to every front of war and raised the morale of his troops by personally speaking to them. He also broadcast many messages through the BBC. He visited the Normandy and Italian battlefields during the World War II.

He visited India also. His countrymen loved him. However, his chain-smoking habit caused him cancer of lungs and he died of it in 1952. George VI won affection of his people by his devotion to duty.

Mihir Sen

India : A Swimming Champion

Born : 1930   Died : 1997

What Mihir Sen achieved in his time in international swimming is significant, although the records he created have been subsequently bettered. In 1966, he established five important records and became an extraordinary salt-water swimmer. He was the first Asian to have crossed the English Channel. In 1959, he was awarded "Padma Shree" and in 1967 "Padma Bhushan".

In 1958, Mihir Sen swam across the English Channel, in 1966 he crossed the Palk Strait, followed by Gibraltar, Dar-E-Daniyal, Wasphorus and Panama. He, thus, established the record of swimming the longest distance.

Mihir Sen was born on 16 November 1930 in Purulia (West Bengal). He was a lawyer by profession, a barrister of the Calcutta High Court. He is a matchless swimmer, having swam more than 600 kilometres in sea/ocean water. He brought glory to his motherland by creating records and earning a place in *Guinness Book of World Record*. He died in 1997 after a brief illness.

P.K. Bannerjee

India : *A Great Football Player*

Born : 1936

Pradeep Kumar Bannerjee gave a new direction to Indian football and established himself as a great and highly respected football player. He started participating in National competitions since 1952 when he was only 16 years old. This is a record in itself. He represented India in 84 matches and scored 60 goals. He was a member of the Indian football team for 12 years. He was the first football player to be awarded "Arjuna" award, which he received in 1961. He considers Indian victory at the Jakarta Asiad as the most significant achievement of his life. He scored five goals in five matches in that event.

Pradeep Kumar Bannerjee had been the mainstay of Indian team. The era of Indian football received a setback in 1966 after his retirement.

Born on 23 June 1936, Bannerjee was fond of football since childhood. His father Prabhat Kumar Bannerjee himself was a great player. Pradeep Bannerjee joined Bihar team for Santosh Trophy in 1952 and reached Olympics through Asiad. After retirement from professional football, he played a very significant role as a celebrated football-coach in Tata Football Academy and in many renowned football clubs at Calcutta like Mohan Bagan, East Bengal and Eastern Railway. He is still very active in the arena of Indian Football as an Advisor. He was also made National Coach of Indian Football for several years.

During the peak hours of his football career, he always remained with his team, Eastern Railway, where he was associated as an high-ranking Railway official. Inspite of lucrative offers received at that time from other renowned football clubs in India, he politely refused to desert his own club, which is still very much near to his heart. ❏❏

David Ben-Gurian

Israel : *Diplomat*

Born : AD 1886   Died : AD1973

Ben-Gurian is to Israel what Mahatma Gandhi is to India. Though Ben-Gurian did not have to struggle for long as did Gandhi but the credit of announcing independence of Israel and getting the British to leave Palestine goes to Ben-Gurian.

Ben-Gurian was born in Poland in the town of Polansk. He had to suffer many hardships and indignities because of being a Jew and it was with great difficulty that he reached Palestine in 1906. He started towards establishing an independent Jewish state almost immediately. He formed the first trade union in Palestine in 1915. When Israel came into being after the First World War, Gurian became the General Secretary of the Israeli Labour Party.

It was his fearless proclamation of independent Jewish State in 1948, that forced the British army to leave Palestine. Thereafter, he became the first Prime Minister of Israel from 1948 to 1953. He again took the reigns of Premiership from 1955 to 1963. He was greatly respected by the leaders of his country and loved by his countrymen. As prime minister, he, more than any other leader, moulded modern Israel.

❏❏

Sir James Chadwick

Britain: Inventor of Neutron

Born : 1891   Died : 1974

The famous British Physicist Sir James Chadwick was born on October 20, 1891 at Manchester. He was awarded Nobel Prize for physics in 1935 for the discovery of neutron. In the early 1900, scientists were aware that atoms contain electrically charged particles called electrons and protons. Scientists also believed that these must be uncharged particles in an atom. In 1932, Chadwick showed that the radiation from the element beryllium, caused by bombardments of alpha particles is actually a stream of electrically neutron particles. He called these particles 'neutrons'. Chadwick also explained the existence of Isotope. An isotope of an element has the same number of protons but different number of neutrons and has therefore a different atomic weight.

Educated at the Universities of Manchestar and Cambridge he also studied under H. Geiger in Berlin. From 1923, he worked with Sir Ernest Rutherford in Cambridge. In 1927, Chadwick was elected a fellow of The Royal Society and in 1932 was awarded the Hughes Medal for his famous discovery. He did pioneering work in the field of nuclear chain reaction. He played an important role in the development of first atomic bomb during World War II.

His discovery provided a new weapon for atomic disintegration, since neutrons, being electrically uncharged, could penetrate undeflected into atomic nucleus.

❏❏

Srinivas Ramanujan

India : Mathematical Wizard

Born : 1887   Died : 1920

Srinivas Ramanujan is among the noted mathematicians of the world. His feats are prodigal. Ramanujan had to face extreme poverty. For many years he was associated with Madras University. In 1914, he went to Cambridge for studies. At that time he was famous as a mathematician. He could solve many difficult questions due to his extraordinary brilliance. In 1917, he became famous in Europe. He returned to India in 1919 and plunged into research. He was selected for Royal Society in 1919 and was the first Indian to be its 'Fellow'.

Ramanujan was born on 22 December 1887 at Erode in Tamil Nadu to extremely poor parents. He always passed his examinations with high marks passing his matriculation at 17. He was married in 1909. He invented new methods for solving mathematical problems. Ramanujan died in Cholpur on 26 April 1920. Many of his works have come to limelight after his death and are being researched upon. During his lifetime even famous British mathematicians were wonderstruck by his genius.

In the short span of 33 years, Ramanujan brought pride to India. The Government of India issued a commemorative stamp in honour of this mathematical wizard. Indian National Science Academy and many other Scientific Institutions in India have established various Medals and Awards in the memory of this great genius.

Shanti S. Bhatnagar

India : The Father of Research Laboratories

Born : AD 1894   **Died : AD 1955**

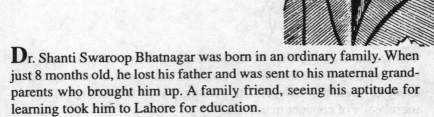

Dr. Shanti Swaroop Bhatnagar was born in an ordinary family. When just 8 months old, he lost his father and was sent to his maternal grandparents who brought him up. A family friend, seeing his aptitude for learning took him to Lahore for education.

He went to England after his M.Sc. on a fellowship. On his return Pt. Madan Mohan Malviya offered him professorship at the Banaras Hindu University. After his day's work, young Bhatnagar used to spend his spare time in his personal laboratory. His laboratory was visited by P.C. Ray and Dr. C.V. Raman. Both appreciated his ingenuity.

Dr. Bhatnagar is remembered for having established various chemical laboratories in the country. He was appointed the Director of Punjab University, Chemistry Department. Meanwhile an Industrial Research Institute was set up in Calcutta and Dr. Bhatnagar was invited to head it. He was awarded the title 'Sir' by the British in recognition of his service to science, in 1941. As Pt Nehru was much in favour of scientific development after independence, Council of Scientific and Industrial Research was set up under the Chairmanship of Dr. Bhatnagar. Later, he was awarded "Padma Bhushan". He became the first Director-General of the Council of Scientific and Industrial Research (CSIR) in 1940 and held this post till his death. After his death, Bhatnagar Memorial Award was instituted by CSIR and other Scientific Organizations in his honour.

Dr. Bhatnagar's life is an example in itself of the fact that talent cannot go waste and that even a man with an ordinary background can shine in life.

❏❏

Acharya J.B. Kripalani

India : Politician

Born : AD 1888   Died : AD 1982

Kripalani came to the forefront of the Indian National Congress leadership by sheer ability and political acumen. He participated in every movement of independence struggle. He was a strong believer in moral code of conduct in politics.

Kripalani participated in 1917 freedom movement. He was jailed for the first time in 1920. He was associated with Gujarat University from 1922-1927 and was called 'Acharya'. He was jailed for 18 months in 1930 for having participated in salt movement. He was jailed for three years for his participation in the Quit India Movement. In 1951, he formed the Kisan Majdoor Dal. He was member of Rajya Sabha and Lok Sabha for many years. He was Secretary of the Indian National Congress and also its President in 1946.

Acharya Kripalani was born in Hyderabad, Sind (now in Pakistan) in a Sindhi family. He did his M.A. from Bombay. From 1912 to 1916 he was a Lecturer in History in Muzzaffarpur, Bihar. He became Private Secretary to Mahamana Malviya in 1918. In 1919, he became Professor of Political Science in Benaras University. He wrote many books also.

He married Sucheta quite late in life. The two had big age difference. Inspite of their political differences they had good relation with each other. Sucheta later became first woman Chief Minister of Uttar Pradesh (1963-67). Sucheta died in the year 1974. Acharya Kripalani was a staunch follower of Mahatma Gandhi. He died in 1982 at 94.

❑❑

Acharya Narendra Dev

India : A Socialist Leader

Born : AD 1889   Died : AD 1956

Acharya Narendra Dev is remembered with great honour among the respected socialists of modern India. He was not only a scholar but a great nationalist and educationist as well. His erudite, frankness and socialist views earned him the respect of Gandhiji and Subhash Bose although they did not entirely subscribe to his views. He was chiefly instrumental in advancing socialism and for this, the labour class considered him as their well-wisher.

Acharya Narendra Dev knew many languages of which Pali, Sanskrit, French and Hindi were main. He was a good writer and an effective orator. His famous book on *Budha Dharma Darshan* has been widely acclaimed. He participated in the non-cooperative movement in 1920. He went to jail many a time. He established the All India Kisan Sabha and was the leader of the Congress Socialist Party established in 1934.

Acharya Narendra Dev was in favour of high moral standards in politics. He was also Vice-Chancellor of Kashi and Lucknow Universities which is a proof of his scholastic capabilities. His spotless clean image as a humanist and ideal personality got him respect from all.

❏❏

T.S. Eliot

England : *Poet and Writer*

Born : AD 1888   **Died : AD 1965**

T.S. Eliot was born in America but he came to England and lived in England all his life. He was educated at various places in England and on the European continent. He knew French and English and was a master of French language, English literature and history.

As is usually the case with writers, Eliot's early works were seen and appreciated by his friends only. He was a teacher in a school for a couple of years and he also served in a bank before shifting fully to literature. He was also the Director of a publishing firm.

Eliot's first poem was published in 1917. Bertrand Russell was the man to spot and recognize his talent. He, along with a couple of his friends, brought Eliot into limelight. In 1922, Eliot got his book *The Wasteland* published, which earned him fame.

Eliot wrote a few plays also. *Murder in a Cathedral* is famous among them. His essays on criticism hold an important place in literature. He received the Order of Merit and the Nobel Prize for literature in 1948. In 1927, he accepted the British citizenship. Eliot is also well known for his free-verses. Among his other works are *Four Quarters* (1944), *The Cocktail Party* (1949), *The Confidential Clerk* (1953) and *The Elder Statesman* (1958). As the editor of *The Criterion* (1922-39) he exercised a moulding influence on the thought of his generation.

Eliot was an intellectual. He gave new trends to the literature and brought in new methods of literary criticism. He was an innovator in this field.

❑❑

Khudi Ram Bose

India : A Young Revolutionary

Born : AD 1889   Died : AD 1908

Bengal has produced many revolutionaries, patriots, nationalists and leaders. Khudi Ram Bose was a revolutionary. For a revolutionary there was no joy in life except the hangman's noose round his neck for the cause of freedom of his motherland. Khudi Ram was a living example of this sacrifice. An inborn patriot, Khudi Ram popularised the gospel of "Vande Mataram" at the tender age of 16. In 1906, at an exhibition organised by the British, he distributed anti-government pamphlets. On 30 April 1908, he and Prafulla Chandra Chaki tried to throw a bomb on the tyrannical magistrate Kingsford, but their plan was thwarted by a few traitors who betrayed them. Khudi Ram was arrested and sentenced to death. He smiled while accepting the hangman's noose.

After his death many patriotic songs were composed highlighting his sacrifice for the cause of motherland which instantly ignited the zeal for freedom among the younger generation of the time.

Khudi Ram Bose was born in Medinapur (West Bengal) on 3 December 1889. He was the only living son of the Bose family. When Khudi Ram was just 6, his parents expired, leaving the child to face untold miseries. In youth, he was drawn to revolutionary activities and he jumped into it heart and soul. He died when only in his teens, on 19 August 1908.

However, the sacrifices of people like Khudi Ram and others did not go in vain. Their dream of a free India materialised, though after a long struggle.

❏❏

Ras Behari Bose

India : A Great Revolutionary

Born : AD 1886   Died : AD 1945

Ras Behari Bose is remembered with reverence as he was one of the great revolutionaries. He was of the opinion that only violent opposition can force the British to leave India. He was a militant. He wanted the British to leave not only India but Asia also.

Ras Behari was involved in 1912 bomb case. He prepared a text called 'Liberty' and distributed it among the public. The British could not apprehend him in the Lahore conspiracy case in 1914 in spite of its best efforts. In 1915, Bose left India for Japan and started preparing his war against the British.

Shri Subhash Chandra Bose was inspired by Ras Behari to form the Azad Hind Army when Subhash went to Japan during the Second World War. He edited *New Asia*, a newsletter and also wrote many books. He also established the 'Indian League' and the 'Indian Independence League'.

Ras Behari was born in a rich family of Bengal. After graduating from Fort Williams College, he started participating in revolutionary activities. He died in Japan in 1945. The Japanese honoured him with "Second Cross Order."

He will always be remembered in India as a leading revolutionary.

❏❏

Chandra Shekhar Azad

India : *A Revolutionary*

Born : AD 1905   Died : AD 1931

Chandra Shekhar Azad will always remain immortal in the annals of history as a man who sacrificed his life on the altar of freedom. At a time when Gandhiji was busy with his Non-Violence Movement to liberate the country, a couple of fiery youngmen were dubious of his methods. They were sure, the best course was to adopt the proverbial policy of 'tit for tat' towards the British. They were in favour of giving the British a befitting reply for their tyranny and injustice. Sardar Bhagat Singh, Sukhdev, Sachindra Sanyal and Ram Prasad Bismil were among those who had no faith in non-violence. While Bhagat Singh was active in Punjab, Chandra Shekhar Azad was busy in UP. He was fired by the zeal to help Bhagat Singh and when the two collaborated, Chandra Shekhar Azad was given the leadership of the activists.

Azad became a member of the group which had vowed to avenge the death of Lala Lajpat Rai. British police officer named Saunders was their target. The group looted Government treasury for funds required for the movement.

Chandra Shekhar Azad was enlisted a terrorist and was under watch. He was a terror to the police. When he was surrounded in Alfred Park, Lucknow, by a strong police squadron, Azad faced them bravely for many hours. Even after his death the British officers dared not approach him. They waited for sometime to confirm his death.

Azad was born at a place called Jhabra in Madhya Pradesh. He ran away from home when young, reached Kashi (Benaras) and joined the freedom struggle when still young. In 1921, he received his first punishment for revolutionary activities. He was sentenced to fifteen lashes. With each stroke of the whip the young patriot shouted "Bharat Mata ki Jai" and thus confounded the officers. He was undaunted and he badly scared the British for the oppression of the Indians.   ❑❑

Ram Prasad Bismil

India : A Great Revolutionary

Born : AD 1897   Died : AD 1927

Ram Prasad Bismil spent his entire life for the cause of India's freedom. At a very early age, he plunged into India's freedom struggle. He took to the armed revolution when Bhai Parmanand was hanged in 1916.

When Ram Prasad was in eighth class, the Indian National Congress session was held in Lucknow. Lokmanya Bal Gangadhar Tilak was also gracing the session. The Congress leaders wanted that Tilak should not be taken through the streets in procession but such was Tilak's popularity that Ram Prasad and his fellows lifted Tilak on their shoulders, seated him in a vehicle and took out the procession.

Ram Prasad Bismil was born in Shahjahanpur. He faced many difficulties in his early years. He came into contact with intellectuals and revolutionaries of Arya Samaj. He was convinced that only an armed struggle can bring India its independence.

Ram Prasad belonged to that state where all kinds of firearms were easily available. He started keeping firearms with him from an early age and also contacted many revolutionaries. He was involved in the 'Mainpuri' and 'Kakokri' conspiracies. In fact, he had planned to rob the state treasury to raise money for purchasing arms and ammunition, but he was caught and sentenced to death by hanging.

To influence and inspire the youth, Ram Prasad Bismil wrote books like *Bolshevik Programme*, *How America Got Independence* and *Swadesh Rang*. He was also a revolutionary poet.

□□

Udham Singh

India : *A Famous Revolutionary*

Born : AD 1899   Died : AD 1940

Udham Singh's name is linked inseparably with Jallianwala Bagh, because he was the man who took his revenge on General O'Dwyer, the British officer who had ordered firing on a peaceful gathering at Amritsar on a Baisakhi Day. Thousands of men, women, children and old men died in the massacre. Many tried to escape by jumping into a nearby well but were suffocated to death. Udham Singh waited for 21 years to avenge this national insult. He killed the villain of the show in England on 13 March 1940. Udham Singh was arrested and sentenced to death on 30 July, the same year.

This fiery revolutionary was born on 18 December 1899 at Sunam in Sangrur District of the Punjab. He was already associated with the struggle for freedom before sailing for England and was sentenced to jail as many as five times for various anti-government activities.

For Udham Singh, the Jallianwala Bagh massacre was a national outrage and ought to have been avenged, so he pledged to take his revenge. In 1937, he reached England after travelling through Europe. In London, he shot General O'Dwyer at a point-blank range in full view of a large gathering.

Udham Singh was all for the unity and solidarity of the country. His life bears a lesson for all those who are propagating divisive ideas in the name of religion.

❏❏

Govind Ballabh Pant

India : *An Able Administrator*

Born : AD 1887   Died : AD 1961

Govind Ballabh Pant was born on 10 December 1887 at Almora in Uttar Pradesh. He was born in a rich family. He was educated mostly at Allahabad. He passed his B.A. in 1907 and law in 1909. He then started practice and earned name, fame and money. He jumped into freedom struggle having been impressed and inspired by the 'non-violent' philosophy of Gokhale, Ranade, Dadabhai Naoroji and Madan Mohan Malviya. He was a leading figure in the Indian freedom movement. He worked mainly in Uttar Pradesh and came into contact with the Nehru family.

Allahabad was the centre of non-violent agitations. In those days burning of foreign clothes, staging sit-in strikes in front of liquor shops and taking out processions in the town were daily occurrences. In one of such procession the Nehru family was also present including Jawahar Lal and Vijaya Laxmi Pandit. Police used horses to trample the processionists and used sticks to beat them. The crowd dispersed. Many fell on the ground. Jawaharlal was also one of them. As a policeman was about to beat him with his baton, Pant threw himself on Jawahar and received all the blows. As a result of this he suffered from ailments for the rest of his life.

Pandit Pant is known as an able administrator. When the Congress formed governments in some states before independence, Pant's abilities came to the forefront. After independence he was made Chief Minister of UP and later for many years was Union Home Minister in the Nehru Cabinet. He had a command over governmental matters. He was a great patriot and was decorated with "Bharat Ratna" in 1957.

❏❏

Rafi Ahmed Kidwai

India : National Leader and Politician

Born : AD 1896   Died : AD 1954

Rafi Ahmed Kidwai was the Food and Agriculture Minister in the Nehru Ministry. During 1952, the prices of wheat suddenly shot up and the dealers started taking advantage of the situation but it was with Rafi Ahmed's presence of mind and efficient handling of the situation that a major catastrophe in the wheat-market was averted. This step gained him great popularity. Even slum-dwellers knew him as a man who saved them their bread.

Rafi Ahmed Kidwai was born at Barabanki in Uttar Pradesh. After his graduation, he joined Gandhiji's Non-cooperation Movement in 1920 and was sent to jail. There, he got to know the Nehrus and acted as Pt. Motilal Nehru's Private Secretary. In 1926, he fought elections as a member of the Swaraj Party, instituted by Motilal Nehru.

In 1936, he was elected President of UP Congress. In 1942, he was again sent to jail for his active participation in Quit India Movement. Thus, his life was dedicated to the country.

It goes to the credit of Rafi Ahmed Kidwai that he was a clean man in politics as well as in his personal dealings. He never took undue advantage of his friendship with the Nehrus, nor did he amass wealth while being a minister. He was, instead, in debt amounting to several thousands at the time of his death. He was a symbol of Hindu-Muslim unity and bred no rancour for anybody though he had suffered a lot during Hindu-Muslim riots. He was above these narrow divisions that separate man from man.

❏❏

Abul Kalam Azad

India : *A Great Patriot & Politician*

Born : AD 1888   Died : AD 1958

Maulana Abul Kalam Azad was a revolutionary from his early days. After finishing his studies, he started *Al-Hilal* an Urdu news magazine. He wanted to bring Muslims into the Congress fold. He was eager to see the end of British rule in India and it was this eagerness that made him join the Bengal revolutionaries.

Abul Kalam was jailed in 1916 for his revolutionary ideas. When Gandhi supported the Khilafat Movement, Abul Kalam became the President of the Khilafat Committee. He was jailed many times between 1920 and 1945. He represented and led the Congress in talks with the British on many occasions. Cripps mission and Simla session in 1945 are some of the examples. He was also made President of the Congress Committee. His contribution to the nationalist movement was immense.

Maulana Azad was born in Mecca. After some years, his family moved to India. He was symbol of Muslim nationalist movement. He was Union Education Minister in the post-independence period. A book *India Wins Freedom*, written by him has been posthumously published, some of whose chapters have controversial opinions about Jawaharlal Nehru. But it is beyond doubt that Abul Kalam was a patriot of the highest order. He was awarded "Bharat Ratna" (posthumous) in the year 1992.

Dr. Zakir Hussain

India : Third President of India

Born : AD 1897   **Died : AD 1969**

Dr Zakir Hussain was one of those nationalist Muslim leaders who followed the Gandhian principles all their lives and who spent a major part of life in fighting for the cause of freedom. He chose the field of education to work for, although he worked with Gandhiji for the upliftment of Harijans, for propagating khadi and such other reconstruction programmes. Gandhiji's programme for basic education, elementary skills and moral education held more appeal to him and he worked wholeheartedly for it. Establishment of the Jamia Millia of Delhi is the result of his efforts.

Dr. Zakir Hussain held high posts after independence, viz. Governor of Bihar in 1957, Vice-President of India in 1962, President of India in 1967. He was also the Vice-Chancellor of Aligarh Muslim University from 1948-56.

As a writer and a staunch believer in Indian culture, Dr Hussain stands out apart. He wrote several books for the reformation and development of Indian education. He was a symbol of secularism. In 1963, he was awarded "Bharat Ratna" in recognition of his services rendered to the nation.

Dr Zakir Hussain was born in Hyderabad in a respectable family. He got his basic education in Aligarh. Later, he went to Germany for higher education. Gandhiji was all praise for the work he did for basic education. He will always be remembered as a great patriot, a social worker and an educationist.

❑❑

General De-Gaulle

France : President of France

Born : AD 1890 **Died : AD 1970**

The name 'De-Gaulle' is synonymous with France. At a time when France was passing through a difficult phase with no stable government running the country, De-Gaulle came to power and brought stability. He is called 'General' because he trained and then led the French army to victory in liberation of France in the Second World War.

In 1940, when Hitler occupied France, De-Gaulle reached England to seek British help. He formed a government-in-exile in London refusing to accept the puppet government set up by Hitler and declared that the Germans will have to vacate France.

De-Gaulle entered Paris in a grand manner in 1944, having forced the Germans to retreat. He became France's Prime Minister in the immediate post-war government. He lost elections in 1946 and for the next 12 years spent life in isolation. That was the period when France was politically unstable. In 1947, he founded a non-party constitutional reform movement and when bankruptcy and civil war loomed large in 1958, he was called to form a government. Thus he returned to power in 1958 and remained its President for 10 years. He brought about the much needed stability in France. During that time he lifted French prestige to great heights and made his own reputation as a world statesman. In 1968, however, a student-worker revolt weakened confidence in De Gaulle's government and on April 28, 1969, he resigned, turning the Fourth Republic Over to Georges Pompidou (1911-1974). His memories covers the war and his years of political power. His other works include *The Army of the Future* (1934).

Every Frenchman feels proud at the mention of De-Gaulle's name.

C. Rajagopalachari

India : First Indian Governor-General of India

Born : 1878   **Died : 1972**

Chakravarti Rajagopalachari, better known as Rajaji was a freedom fighter, statesman, scholar, thinker, humorist and humanist. Along with Gandhi, Nehru and Patel, he was one of the strong pillars of the Indian National Congress. After independence he succeeded Lord Mountbatten as the Governor-General of India. Born on December 10, 1878, in Thorapalli village in Hosur Taluka of Salem district to Chakravarti Iyengar and singaramma, C. Rajagopalachari had graduated from the Presidency College, Madras. He took his B.L. Degree in 1899. After getting his degree in law he started practice in Salem in 1900, and soon reached the peak of glory in his profession. He won practically all his cases. Rajaji had met Gandhiji in 1919 and like the latter he was upset by the Rowlatt Committee recommendations. Later he became Gandhiji's lieutenant in the south. During freedom struggle, Rajaji was lodged in jail several times.

Rajaji also organised a successful Flag Satyagraha in Nagpur in 1923. Like Gandhiji he too broke Salt Laws on April 13, 1930, by leading a 150 mile march of 98 Satyagrahis from Trichy to Vedarnyam. Rajaji played a leading part in shaping the Poona Pact. He had the unique ability of resolving differences between Hindus and Muslims and for that reason he was made the Governor of Bengal after independence. Later when the term of Lord Mountbatten ended, Rajaji was made the first Indian Governor-General of India. He was awarded the Bharat Ratna in 1954.

Ramakrishna Paramahansa

India : The Spiritual Holy Soul!

Born : 1936   Died 1886

Born in a poor Brahmin family in the Hooghly District, West Bengal, Gadadhar Chatterjee (Chottopadhyaya) began showing unusual sign of religious ecstasy when he was only a mere child. At the age of 19, after his marriage with Sarada Devi, Gadadhar came to Calcutta to live with his elder brother to succeed the priesthood of Dakshineswar Kali Temple, established by Rani Rashmoni. From there itself he came to be called "Ramakrishna" as a devotee of Goddess Kali. Visions, trances, ecstasies crowded upon him and most of his time was spent in intense spiritual activities. He proceeded under various spiritual guides to experience the whole gamut of mystical relationship described in Hindu scriptures ranging from intense emotional raptures to the supreme beatitude of *Nirvikara Samadhi*.

By sheer force of his spiritual attainment, Ramakrishna became Paramahansa, the beacon light in the encircling gloom of his time. Gradually the fame of this unlettered young priest began to spread and people from all walks of life began finding their way to visit him.

Ramakrishna reaffirmed on the basis of his own spiritual experiments that all creeds and religions led ultimately to the same goal. He also proceeded to adopt the spiritual practices of Christianity as well as Islam. He exhorted people not to waste time squabbling over this or that religion but to seek God with pure and dedicated heart. He expressed his teachings in a series of homely and telling parables that made them intelligible to even the most common villager. His sayings and story of his life remain to this day a major source of religious guidelines.

Under his great influence he attracted to him a group of young disciples. They found Ramakrishhna a source of tremendous inspiration. Outstanding among them was young Narendra Nath Dutta—later to be famous world over as Swamy Vivekananda.

V. Shantaram

India: *Film Producer and Director*

Bordn: AD 1901   Died: AD 1990

Shantaram Rajaram Vankudre has a special place in the Indian film industry. Apart from being a producer-director, he also acted in few films. His contribution to the Indian film industry is immeasurable. *Saavkari Paash* was his first film. Social order, exploitation and music and dance were his forte. He also produced a documentary on Cripps mission. He was a pioneer in many an improvement in film production. He was first to use zoom lens, first to produce a children's film and first to produce a colour film in the country. *Maya Bazaar*, 1923; *Dr Kotnis Ki Amar Kahani*, 1946; *Admi*, 1939, *Shakuntala*, 1943; *Jhanak-Jhanak Payal Baaze*, 1955; *Geet Gaya Patharon Ne*, 1964; *Boond Jo Ban Gaye Moti*, 1967; *Chaani*, 1977 are some of his immortal films.

Shantaram was born on 18 November 1901 at Kolhapur in Maharashtra in a poor family. He had to do odd jobs to earn livelihood even in childhood. But he attained success with his struggle and efforts. He formed the Prabhat Film Company in 1929. He was immortalised by *Netaji Palkar*, *Gopal Krishna* and *Duniya Naa Mane*. He came to Bombay in 1941 and established the Rajkamal Kala Mandir Studio.

For his immense contribution to the films world, he was awarded 'Dadasaheb Phalke Award' in 1986. He died on 27 October, 1990.

❏❏

Enricho Fermi

Italy : A Scientist of Atomic Energy

Born : AD 1901   Died : AD 1954

Fermi was a brilliant scientist. He was born in Rome, Italy on 29 September 1901. He was inclined towards science from the very beginning. Apart from his textbooks he read so much that by the time he reached college, he had acquired so much knowledge about physics that was greater than his teacher.

By that time, atom had become an important part of Physics. Marie Curie, Rutherford, and other scientists had done lot of research work on atomic theory and it was well known that atomic energy has vast scope for development. Fermi chose this as his research subject. He did lot of experiments on radium. He was awarded the Noble Prize in 1938. However, he left Italy alongwith his wife when he went to Stockholm to receive the Nobel Prize. He did not agree with the policies of Dictator Mussolini and his friend Hitler. He therefore, came to America.

Nothing better could have happened to America. It wanted to go ahead with the establishment of an atomic reactor and take full advantage of the developments of atomic energy. Who else than Fermi for this? He was entrusted with the job and was successful in it in 1942. Fermi built the first atomic reactor in an empty squash court in Chicago. He set off here the first man-made nuclear chain reaction. Later he helped to develop the atom bomb.

In spite of being extremely busy, Fermi found time to play tennis and do skiing. He died in 1954.

❏❏

Dr M. S. Swaminathan

India : Agricultural Scientist

Born : AD 1925

Dr M.S. Swaminathan is not only a famous scientist but also an able administrator and an efficient organiser of projects. He has served the country by holding many significant positions. His researches in the field of agriculture and his efforts for improving the quality of wheat in particular, have won him laurels. Dr Borlogue has highly appreciated his works. He is regarded as the father of India's Green Revolution.

Dr Swaminathan was born in Kumbakonam, a village in Tamil Nadu. Dr Swaminathan has spent a lifetime in the field of agriculture and food-production. He worked at home and abroad. He worked as the Director of Pusa Institute; Director General of Indian Agriculture Research Council; Secretary, Ministry of Agriculture and Vice-Chairman of the Planning Commission. He is a well-wisher of the farmers and has always had their welfare in mind. Swaminathan also was the Director-General of International Rice Research Institute, Manila.

Dr Swaminathan is an honorary member of several important National and International Scientific Societies/Councils including the Royal Society of London. Many Universities have conferred doctorate on him. In 1972, he was awarded "Padma Bhushan" and won Magsaysay Award in 1971. He was the Leader of Indian delegation at the International Genetic Congress, U.K. in 1993. Dr Swaminathan believes in work, not in popularity and that is the reason he never came into so much limelight.

He is the pride and glory of our country. Dr Swaminathan presently heads "The Centre for Research on Sustainable Agriculture and Rural Development" at Madras.

Guru Tegh Bahadur

India : The Symbol of Righteousness

Born : 1623 Died : 1675

Guru Tegh Bhadur—the 9th occupant of Guru Nanak's holy seat felt that it was his duty for right causes, to stem the tide of persecution led by Aurangzeb—the Mogul Emperor, against Hindu and other non-Muslim population. What Aurangzeb aimed at was to make India into Islamic dominion, where all vestiges of ancient Indian culture were to be obliterated by the rising tide of Islamic zeal. Guru Tegh Bahadur viewing with deep anguish the tyranny let loose all over the land, set out on a mission to lead the oppressed people in their resolve to adhere to their cherished spiritual values, their *Dharma* and culture to plead with the Emperor. He demanded to treat the various classes of the Indian society with proper justice.

He was however arrested, arraigned before the court of Muslim Clergymen as a rebel and enemy of Islam, and offered, as was used in such cases, the choice between Islam and death. The brave Guru naturally refused to apostate himself and act in a craven manner to save his own life. In 1675, he was beheaded after being severely tortured in the Chandni Chowk of Delhi, at a stone's throw from Red Fort—the Royal residence. At the spot of his martyrdom, which was then a prison, stands now a magnificent Sikh monument, the Sisganj Gurudwara.

Guru established his capital at Anandpur, where he founded the new community—Khalsa (literally, community of the pure), appointed five people from his followers, who had undergone severe bravery test by the Guru before their attainment. They were called Singh or Lion. So, in theory every Sikh thereafter is called Singh. It was his reform which set Sikhism on the path of both a military and a religious power. Later, his son Guru Govind Singh recorded his regards to his father which reads as follows:"The Master performed the supreme sacrifice to cherish God's devotees and gave up his head, but not his passion for righteousness".

Satyajit Ray

India: The Genius Indian Film Maker

Born : 1921 **Died : 1992**

The Indian cinema started in 1913 with the release of the silent film Raja Harischandra made by Dada Saheb Phalke. However, Alam Ara became the first sound film in 1931. During 1930s Indian cinema stories had themes of social protests and generally was confined to romantic, historical and mythological themes. But the big turning point to Indian cinema came in 1955 taking it at par with International standards by the legendary genius filmmaker Satyajit Ray.

Ray was born in Calcutta. He started his career as a commercial artist before making films. His first feature film "Pather Panchali" (The song of the Road). This film was his most notable one for its realistic potrayal of everyday life and artistic composition of his camera work that earned him worldwide recognition. He received many prestigious International/National awards for creation of this master piece.

Satyajit Ray had a special vision of Indian reality—hard but unbearably truthful yet moving. He was not just a great cine director but had superb mastery over other related cinematic work. He was a great writer, good composer and one of the best dialogue writers. Ray composed the music for most of his films. He made 28 full length feature films and a few documentaries. Among his most famous films *Pather Panchali, Apajito, Apur Sansar, Charulata, Goopy Gyne Bagha Byne, Shatranj ke Khiladi* (Hindi), *Sadgati* (Telefilm), *Nayak* and *Aagantuk* occupy a special place in the hearts of cine lovers.

His films got wide popularity especially in USA and France. The French Government awarded him "The Legion of Honour"—the highest award in France. He also received many awards like the Magsaysay award (1967) and Dada Saheb Phalke award (1984). He was decorated with "Bharat Ratna" in 1992. But the happiest moment in his life came when he was informed in his death bed of winning the special Oscar Award.

Birju Maharaj

India : A Kathak Dance Wizard

Born : AD 1938

If one were to refer to Kathak Dance, the name to be conjured with will be Birju Maharaj. It is he who has established Kathak as a classical dance-form. He is a great *guru* who has produced renowned artists, evolved different styles and new traditions. Kathak dance form flowered due to his efforts. If it is popular and respected today, the credit goes to Birju Maharaj.

His efficiency and ability gained for Birju Maharaj great respect. At 22, he received the prestigious national award for the Central Sangeet Natak Academy. He was given "Padma Bhushan". Madhya Pradesh government awarded him the "Kalidas Samman", the highest in the field of fine-arts. He is a combination of an efficient dancer, a singer and a player of instruments. He has been abroad and has been hailed as a dancer with extraordinary abilities.

Born on 4 February 1938, Birju Maharaj belongs to a family with a sound background in dancing. His father Acchhan Maharaj was also a dancer. He spent his childhood in Rampur, Patiala and Raigarh and was fortunate in being in an atmosphere conducive to his talent. His stage performances earned him name and appreciation when he was young which served as an inspiration to him. Behind his success, however, there is unflinching perseverance, hard work and talent.

Birju Maharaj has dedicated his life to his art. He is the guiding light to newcomers in the field. He is an able choreographer. Kathak Dance form will always display his influence. In 1957, his Kathak dance-drama "Malati Madhavan" along with Lachhu Maharaj was dedicated to the memory of Wajid Ali Shah and still remains in the permanent repertoire of Bhartiya Kala Kendra. He has been the Director and *Guru* at Centre for the Kathak in New Delhi.

❏❏

Amrita Pritam

India : Punjabi Author of World Fame

Born : AD 1919   Died : AD 2005

Amrita Pritam is one of the great writers of modern India. A Gyanpeeth award winner for 1983 for her *Kagaz te Kanvas* (Punjabi), Amrita Pritam has authored more than 60 books. Her works have been translated in as many as 30 languages. Besides Punjabi, she has mastery over Hindi and Urdu. She was nominated as a member of Rajya Sabha in 1986. She is popular outside India also. Her autobiography is entitled *Rasidi Ticket* (Revenue Stamp). Some of her other famous works are *Dekha Kabira*, *Kadi Dhoop Ka Safar*, *Dastavej*, *Therhawa Suraj*, *Dilli Ki Galian*. Her recently published second autobiography is *Shadows of Words*. She was a member of the Press Council in 1980.

Amrita Pritam's life is as good or bad as an open book. She is frank about her views on marriage. Talking about her first marriage and her relations with Imroz, she admits that marriage is a futile and outdated institution. Her name is Amrita. While Pritam is her ex-husband's name. Amrita Pritam's readers can vouchsafe the similarity between her life and her works. She has widely travelled and covered almost half the world. She has tried to beautify literature by her works and hopes to continue adding to it.

Her personal life can be summed up in Pablo Neruda's words — "My house has two doors — one opens inside towards myself, the other opens outside towards the troubles and tribulations of the people. These doors shall ever remain open".

Joseph Priestly

England : Inventor of Oxygen

Born : AD 1733 **Died : AD 1804**

The world today spends millions and trillions of rupees on aerated drinks like Coca-Cola. Did Joseph Priestly know that by mixing carbon-dioxide in water he would be giving the world a new business and that a transaction in millions would ensue? He was awarded a gold medal for this invention. But, the discovery of Soda-water is not Priestly's only contribution to science. He is particularly known in the field for the discovery of life-giving gas, oxygen apart from other gases like ammonia, carbon monoxide and hydrogen-sulphide. He discovered that green plants require sunlight and give off oxygen.

Priestly was born in England in a village near Leeds on 13 March 1733. His father was a poor weaver. Orphaned when just seven, Joseph was brought by his aunt. For sustenance he worked in a small Church just on a very meagre salary. But, since this was not enough, he took tuitions and wrote books to earn whatever he could. He, however, continued his study of languages and chemistry. During Benjamin Franklin's visit to England, Priestly met him and the two developed a life-long friendship. Franklin was an American and was in England for mustering public opinion for the independence of American colonies. Influenced by Franklin, Priestly wrote a book *The History of the Present Condition of Electricity*. His association in 1780's with "Lunar Society" brought him into contact with scientists like James Watt, and Erasmus Darwin.

He held the view that religion and politics should have clearly demarcated boundaries which should not be over-lapping. Excited by his unconventional ideas an angry mob set his house on fire on 14 July 1781, and his works of the past twenty years in the field of science were burnt down to ashes in a couple of minutes. Priestly and his family, however, escaped the catastrophe as they were not at home then. He died at the age of 71.

Amrita Shergill

India : An Artist

Born : AD 1913   Died : AD 1956

The credit for modernising art in India goes to Amrita Shergill. Her works display an assimilation of Indian and Western art. Amrita Shergill, who gave new dimensions to Indian art, was herself influenced by Mughal and Rajasthani style. The many art exhibitions she held gave impetus to her art. Her best known paintings are: *An Ancient story-teller*, *Three Virgins*, *The Celibate*.

Amrita Shergill was born on January 30, 1913 at Budapest (Hungary). In 1929, she came to India and stayed in Shimla. Prior to that she had completed her education in Paris with music and painting. After a visit abroad, she came back to India in 1934. Pandit Jawaharlal Nehru was much impressed by her art. In 1936, she made a self-portrait which became the talk of the time. In 1938, she married Victor Allen, a Hungarian. Her married life was beset with many financial difficulties. Amrita Shergill died on 5 December 1956 at Lahore. It was an untimely demise.

Amrita Shergill's works, which gave a new light to Indian painting, are admired for their depth and innovative skills. National Museum of Arts houses her pieces in a separate room. Nudes in Indian painting were brought in by her which is a clear case of Western influence. In her short span of life she has left a rich legacy to Indian painting.

❏❏

List of Personalities in *World-Famous* 101 Great Lives Vol. 1

Indira Gandhi	Garfield Sobers	Leo Tolstoy
Adolf Hitler	Prakash Padukone	Florence Nightingale
Albert Einstein	Wilhelm K. Roentgen	Mao Tse-tung
Mother Teresa	William Gilbert Grace	Charlie Chaplin
Plato	Sir J.C. Bose	Raja Ram Mohan Roy
Rabindranath Tagore	Swami Vivekananda	Alexander Dumas
Salim Ali	Pele	Martin Luther King
Kapil Dev	George Bernard Shaw	Daniel Defoe
Homer	Mahavir Swami	'Osho' Rajneesh
Alexander The Great	Alfred Nobel	Abraham Lincoln
Jawaharlal Nehru	Pablo Picasso	Dr. H.J. Bhabha
Tulsidas	Abdul Gaffar Khan	George Washington
Sir Arthur Conan Doyle	Lenin	Tenzing Norgay
Tansen	Charles Darwin	Ernest Hemingway
Gautama Buddha	Lala Lajpat Rai	Chanakya
Louis Pasteur	Bal Gangadhar Tilak	Queen Victoria
Mirza Ghalib	Rani Luxmi Bai	Charles Dickens
Socrates	Chiang Kai-Shek	Napoleon Bonaparte
Karl Marx	William Shakespeare	Julius Caesar
Maxim Gorky	Subhash Chandra Bose	Vasco da Gama
Sir Isaac Newton	Sir C.V. Raman	Lata Mangeshkar
Ravi Shankar	Morrison Tony	Agatha Christie
V.S. Naipaul	Henry Ford	John F. Kennedy
Jesus Christ	Walt Disney	Lewis Carroll
Donald Bradman	Jesse Owens	Aristotle
Leonardo da Vinci	Akbar The Great	George Stephenson
Sardar Vallabhbhai Patel	Erwin Rommel	Sardar Bhagat Singh
Dhyan Chand	W.A. Mozart	Kalidasa
Sir Winston Churchill	J. Krishnamurti	Prem Chand
Sunil Gavaskar	Dr. B.R. Ambedkar	Prophet Mohammed
Thomas Alva Edison	Guru Nanak	Ashoka The Great
Milkha Singh	Bobby Fischer	Zarathustra
P.T. Usha	Moses	Johnn Sebastian Bach
Mahatma Gandhi	Yuri Gagarin	

List of Personalities in *World-Famous* 101 Great Lives Vol. 3

Alfred Dreyfus	Niepce	Solomon
Benito Mussolini	Shakuntala Devi	Chandragupta-II
Chou En-Lai	Vikram Sarabhai	Douglas McArthur
Colonel Nasser	Christopher Columbus	Lord William Bentinck
Dr S. Ramgoolam	Fa-hsien	Maharana Pratap
Giuseppe Garibaldi	Marco Polo	Razia Sultan
Ho Chi Minh	David Ricardo	Samudragupta
Jean-Paul Sartre	Gunnar Myrdal	Ben Johnson
Joseph Stalin	John D. Rockefeller	Bruce Lee
Josip Broz Tito	Thomas Robert Malthus	Chris Evert Lloyd
Lal Bahadur Shastri	Aesop	Christine Otto
Metternich	Alfred Hitchcock	Fanny Blankers
Mazzini Giuseppe	Dante Alighieri	Frank Mike Tyson
Margaret Thatcher	Faiz Ahmad 'Faiz'	Ivan Lendl
Mohammad Reza Pahlavi	Goethe	Nadia Comaneci
Mikhail S. Gorbachev	James Hadley Chase	Martin Frost
Nelson Mandela	Jim Corbett	Richard Hadlee
Nietzsche	John Dryden	Sebastian Coe
Dr. Rajendra Prasad	Omar Khayyam	Sergei Bubka
Rajiv Gandhi	Salman Rushdie	Amitabh Bachchan
Ronald Reagan	Shaikh Sadi	Igor F. Stravinsky
Saddam Hussein	Joan of Arc	Kishore Kumar
Andrey D. Sakharov	Victor Hugo	Zubin Mehta
Arthur Schopenhauer	Voltaire	Marilyn Monroe
Bob Geldof	Henry Moore	Marlon Brando
Hegel	Marc Chagall	Mukesh
John Stuart Mill	Michelangelo	Raj Kapoor
Maria Montessori	Vincent Van Gogh	Michael Jackson
Niccolo Machiavelli	Christine Keeler	Sean Connery
Jean Jacques Rousseau	Cleopatra	Sophia Loren
Sigmund Freud	Jacqueline Kennedy	Dalai Lama
Benjamin Franklin	Madonna	Confucius
Louis Braille	Princess Diana	Martin Luther
Michael Faraday	Rasputin	

Rapidex Courses & General Knowledge

Adopted by CRORES of Readers in India & abroad

Price: 110/- each

The course is available separately in: **Hindi, Gujarati, Telugu, Tamil, Marathi, Bangla, Kannada, Nepali, Malayalam, Assamese, Oriya, Gurmukhi, Urdu and Arabic.**

FREE Audio cassette

Rapidex Language Learning Course
A 12-Volume series teaching 6 Regional Languages through Hindi & vice versa

Price: 75/- each

Hindi Learning Courses through Regional Languages	Regional Language Learning Courses through Hindi
Bangla-Hindi	Hindi-Bangla
Gujarati-Hindi	Hindi-Gujarati
Malayalam-Hindi	Hindi-Malayalam
Tamil-Hindi	Hindi-Tamil
Kannada-Hindi	Hindi-Kannada
Telugu-Hindi	Hindi-Telugu

Rapidex Computer Course
A step-by-step self learning kit

Price: 196/- each

FREE GIFTS: Tutorial CD, Mouse Pad & SMS Language Book

Children's Knowledge Bank
A tonic to your child's brain

SAVE 20% Pay Rs. 300/- instead of Rs. 360/- for complete set of 6 vols. priced Rs. 60/- each

Children's Science Library

SAVE 20% Pay Rs. 350/- instead of Rs. 425/- for complete set of 17 books priced Rs.25/- each

Price: 96/-

Rapidex **DTP Course**

Price: 150/- each

Easiest and simplest way to make useful projects...

71 New Science Projects Self-Learning Kit

Price: 120/- each

FREE CD

Rapidex **SELF LETTER DRAFTING COURSE**
Instant Letter Producer
Fully revised edition — Over 10,00,000 copies sold

Price: 110/-

Self-improvement

104 pp • Rs. 60/-

376 pp • Rs. 120/-

240 pp • Rs. 96/-

136 pp • Rs. 96/-

240 pp • Rs. 120/-

120 pp • Rs. 80/-
Also available in Hindi

155 pp • Rs. 80/-

156 pp • Rs. 80/-

192 pp • Rs. 96/-

160 pp • Rs. 96/-

140 pp • Rs. 80/-

144 pp • Rs. 80/-

64 pp • Rs. 60/-
Also available in Hindi

136 pp • Rs. 68/-
Also available in Hindi

168 pp • Rs. 120/-

96 pp • Rs. 68/-

112 pp • Rs. 80/-

80 pp • Rs. 60/-
Also available in Hindi

160 pp • Rs. 68/-
Also available in Hindi

192 pp • Rs. 96/-

176 pp • Rs. 68/-

218 pp • Rs. 80/-

174 pp • Rs. 80/-

192 pp • Rs. 80/-

184 pp • Rs. 96/-

Self-Improvement, Hobbies & Quotations

0 pp • Rs. 88/-

140 pp • Rs. 60/-

180 pp • Rs. 80/-

112 pp • Rs. 95/-

192 pp • Rs. 195/-

8 pp • Rs. 96/-

312 pp • Fs. 160/-

128 pp • Rs. 60/-

176 pp • Rs. 60/-

304 pp • Rs. 120/-

8 pp • Rs. 80/-

176 pp • Rs. 80/-

176 pp • Rs. 68/-

176 pp • Rs. 80/-

128 pp • Rs. 120/-

8 pp • Rs. 80/-

120 pp • Rs. 60/-
Also available in Hindi

124 pp • Rs. 68/-
Also available in Hindi

64 pp • Rs. 50/-

64 pp • Rs. 50/-

6 pp • Rs. 68/-

144 pp • Rs. 68/-

96 pp • Rs. 60/-

128 pp • Rs. 80/-

128 pp • Rs. 96/-

Career & Management

160 pp • Rs. 80/-
Also available in Hindi

144 pp • Rs. 80/-

160 pp • Rs. 68/-

172 pp • Rs. 99/-

136 pp • Rs. 96/-

128 pp • Rs. 96/-

100 pp • Rs. 150/-

144 pp • Rs. 96/-

128 pp • Rs. 80/-

120 pp • Rs. 80/-

392 pp • Rs. 60/-

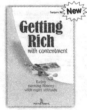
144 pp • Rs. 96/-

200 pp • Rs. 88/-

200 pp • Rs. 88/-

106 pp • Rs. 80/-

248 pp • Rs. 150/-

336 pp • Rs. 175/-

192 pp • Rs. 150/-

128 pp • Rs. 80/-

120 pp • Rs. 75/-
Earlier printed as Teens to Twenties

240 pp • Rs. 195/-

176 pp • Rs. 150/-

96 pp • Rs. 96/-

472 pp • Rs. 450/-

280 pp • Rs. 135/-

Career & Management / Popular Science

62 pp • Rs. 120/-

424 + Maps pp • Rs. 150/-

136 pp • Rs. 80/-

184 pp • Rs. 88/-

138 pp • Rs. 80/-

00 pp • Rs. 68/-

128 pp • Rs. 95/-

256 pp • Rs. 120/-

152 pp • Rs. 96/-

160 pp • Rs. 72/-

36 pp • Rs. 68/-

160/- pp • Rs. 80/-

208 pp • Rs. 88/-

280 pp • Rs. 195/-

188 pp • Rs. 220/-

76 pp • Rs. 68/-

136 pp • Rs. 80/-

120 pp • Rs. 68/-

288 pp • Rs. 96/-

in press
Sentence Corrections for GMAT

296 pp • Rs. 150/-

120 pp each
Rs. 60/- each

144 pp • Rs. 60/-

104 pp each
Rs. 36/- each

Health, Yogasana & Body Fitness

 128 pp • Rs. 60/-
 152 pp • Rs. 96/-
 224 pp • Rs. 120/-
 224 pp • Rs. 150/-
 192 pp • Rs. 96/-

 112 pp • Rs. 60/-
 115 pp • Rs. 80/-
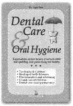 136 pp • Rs. 68/-
 120 pp • Rs. 80/-
 104 pp • Rs. 69/-

 232 pp • Rs. 90/-
 144 pp • Rs. 80/-
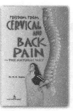 128 pp • Rs. 60/-
 224 pp • Rs. 135/-
 168 pp • Rs. 88/-

 136 pp • Rs. 68/-
 304 pp • Rs. 120/-
 144 pp • Rs. 80/-
 52 pp • Rs. 24/-
 152 pp • Rs. 80/-

 126 pp • Rs. 80/-
 428 pp • Rs. 175/-
 312 pp • Rs. 120/-
 140 pp • Rs. 96/- (Vol. I)
 224 pp • Rs. 135/- (Vol. II)

Health, Yogasana & Body Fitness

128 pp • Rs. 96/-

136 pp • Rs. 68/-

96 pp • Rs. 40/-

112 pp • Rs. 60/-
Also available in Hindi

128 pp • Rs. 48/-
Also available in Hindi

96 pp • Rs. 48/-

112 pp • Rs. 60/-
(Also available in Hindi)

120 pp • Rs. 60/-

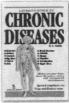
176 pp • Rs. 96/-

192 pp • Rs. 96/-

224 pp • Rs. 88/-

200 pp • Rs. 80/-
Also available in Hindi

168 pp • Rs. 80/-

272 pp • Rs. 195/-

224 pp • Rs. 80/-

96 pp • Rs. 80/-

132 pp • Rs. 96/-

128 pp • Rs. 60/-

192 pp • Rs. 68/-

228 pp • Rs. 120/-

152 pp • Rs. 80/-

176 pp • Rs. 96/-

128 pp • Rs. 68/-

184 pp • Rs. 96/-

124 pp • Rs. 96/-

Alternative Therapies

136 pp • Rs. 60/-

64 pp • Rs. 48/-

144 pp • Rs. 80/-

240 pp • Rs. 88/-

84 pp • Rs. 48/-

168 pp • Rs. 80/-

224 pp • Rs. 80/-

200 pp • Rs. 96/-

180 pp • Rs. 68/-

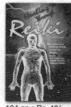
104 pp • Rs. 48/-

120 pp • Rs. 60/-

128 pp • Rs. 68/-

200 pp • Rs. 80/-

128 pp • Rs. 68/-

242 pp • Rs. 96/-

280 pp • Rs. 88/-

304 pp • Rs. 120/-

264 pp • Rs. 135/-

112 pp • Rs. 80/-

112 pp • Rs. 68/-

264 pp • Rs. 108/-

144 pp • Rs. 80/-

168 pp • Rs. 96/-

112 pp • Rs. 68/-

144 pp • Rs. 60/-

Palmistry, Hypnotism, Astrology & Numerology

264 pp • Rs. 120/-

184 pp • Rs. 80/-

144 pp • Rs. 80/-

264 pp • Rs. 110/-

200 pp • Rs. 96/-

144 pp • Rs. 60/-

136 pp • Rs. 80/-

248 pp • Rs. 135/-

160 pp • Rs. 68/-

152 pp • Rs. 80/-

336 pp • Rs. 195/-
Hardbound

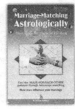
142 pp • Rs. 80/-

272 pp • Rs. 96/-

222 pp • Rs. 80/-

120 pp • Rs. 68/-

282 pp • Rs. 88/-

180 pp • Rs. 80/-

236 pp • Rs. 75/-
Also available in Hindi

365 pp • Rs. 80/-
Also available in Hindi

272 pp • Rs. 88/-

107 pp • Rs. 80/-

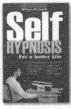
184 pp • Rs. 88/-

160 pp • Rs. 60/-
Also available in Hindi

92 pp • Rs. 60/-

Dictionaries, Encyclopedias & Story Books

128 pp • Rs. 60/-

58 pp • Rs. 72/-

98 pp • Rs. 72/-

152 pp • Rs. 24/-

231 pp • Rs. 120/-

196 pp • Rs. 60/-

48 pp • Rs. 48/-

136 pp • Rs. 50/-

136 pp • Rs. 60/-

Bloomsbury Dictionaries

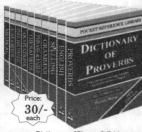

Price: 30/- each

- Dictionary of Phrase & Fable
- English Thesaurus
- Spelling Dictionary
- Dictionary of English Usage
- Medical Dictionary
- Dictionary of Calories
- English Dictionary
- Dictionary of Grammar
- Dictionary of Proverbs
- Dictionary of Quotations

520 pp • Rs. 380/-

344 pp • Rs. 120/-

128 pp • Rs. 68/-

220 pp • Rs. 80/-

3 Vols. • pp: 24 each • Rs. 36/- each
Also available in Hindi

2 Vols. • pp: 56 & 60 each
Rs. 60/- each
Also available in Hindi

2 Vols. • pp: 56 each
Rs. 60/- each
Also available in Hindi

120 pp
Rs. 48/-

96 pp
Rs. 48/-

24 pp • Rs. 36/-
Also in Hindi

60 pp • Rs. 60/-
Also in Hindi

48 pp • Rs. 50/-
Also in Hindi

5 Vols. • pp: 60 to 68 each
Rs. 60/- each
Also available in Hindi

Combined Edition
pp: 304 • Rs. 350/-
Also available in Hindi

Computer & Quiz Books

144 pp • Rs. 95/-

136 pp • Rs. 99/-

264 pp • Rs. 80/-

360/- pp • Rs. 195/-

192 pp • Rs. 68/-

416 pp • Rs. 195/-

444 pp • Rs. 225/-

392 pp • Rs. 225/-

184 pp • Rs. 90/-

252 pp • Rs. 125/-

296 pp • Rs. 140/-

164 pp • Rs. 120/-

Rapidex Straight to the Point Series

Price: 60/- each

Rapidex Condensed Users Guides

Price: 140/- each

448 pp • Rs. 175/-

520 pp • Rs. 195/-

240 pp • Rs. 88/-

208 pp • Rs. 60/-

128 pp • Rs. 60/-

260 pp • Rs. 60/-

176 pp • Rs. 60/-

256 pp • Rs. 96/-

232 pp • Rs. 60/-

216 pp • Rs. 60/-

192 pp • Rs. 48/-

208 pp • Rs. 80/-

192 pp • Rs. 60/-

128 pp • Rs. 60/-

Parenting, Pre-school, Love, Sex & Romance

232 pp • Rs. 120/-

240 pp • Rs. 88/-

52 pp • Rs. 100/-
Also available in Hindi

120 pp • Rs. 60/-

160 pp • Rs. 80/-

118 pp • Rs. 75/-

193 pp • Rs. 80/-

120 pp • Rs. 88/-

116 pp • Rs. 60/-

144 pp • Rs. 60/-

100 pp • Rs. 60/-

136 pp • Rs. 80/-

204 pp • Rs. 68/-

64 pp • Rs. 30/-

120 pp • Rs. 60/-

136 pp • Rs. 60/-

150 pp • Rs. 68/-

144 pp • Rs. 80/-

160 pp • Rs. 40/-

128 pp • Rs. 80/-

24 pp • Rs. 36/-

Rs. 15/- each
Fully coloured
& illustrated.
Can be wiped off.

208 pp • Rs. 135/-

Cookery, Women Orientation, Beauty

| 102 pp • Rs. 60/- | 136 pp • Rs. 80/- | 152 pp • Rs. 125/- | 104 pp • Rs. 60/- | 86 pp • Rs. 80/- | 96 pp • Rs. 96/- |

| 144 pp • Rs. 68/- Also available in Hindi | 120 pp • Rs. 80/- | 112 pp • Rs. 60/- | 144 pp • Rs. 60/- | 140 pp • Rs. 60/- | 86 pp • Rs. 60/- |

| 192 pp • Rs. 96/- | 248 pp • Rs. 96/- | 296 pp • Rs. 150/- | 32 pp each • Rs. 40/- each |

| 152 pp • Rs. 110/- | 112 pp • Rs. 80/- | 128 pp • Rs. 80/- Also available in Hindi |

| 128 pp • Rs. 68/- | 144 pp • Rs. 75/- Also available in Hindi | 124 pp • Rs. 60/- |

COOKERY (a set of 4 books)

you save 20%
Pay Rs. 200/- instead of Rs. 240/- for complete set of 4 books priced Rs. 60/- each
Demy size books.

- 101 Mix & Match Recipes with Vegetables
- 101 Chinese Recipes
- 101 Ways to Prepare Curries
- 101 Ways to Prepare Soups & Salads

Humour, Fun, Facts, Magic & Mysteries

50 Wittiest Tales of Birbal	Amusing Anecdotes on Indian Red Tape	Armour of Humour	Deft Definitions	Medical Jokes & Humour	Over a Cup of Coffee
120 pp • Rs. 48/-	176 pp • Rs. 80/-	128 pp • Rs. 40/-	120 pp • Rs. 48/-	168 pp • Rs. 48/-	244 pp • Rs. 120/-

Rib-Tickling Jokes — 128 pp • Rs. 60/-
Stories from Panchatantra — 115 pp • Rs. 60/-
The Funniest Tales of Mullah Nasruddin — 144 pp • Rs. 48/- Also in Hindi
The World's Best Professional Jokes — 120 pp • Rs. 60/-
The World's Best Thought-Provoking Jokes — 176 pp • Rs. 80/-
Unwritten Flaws of Indian Bureaucracy — 248 pp • Rs. 295/- (Hardbound)

101 Brain Teasers — 152 pp • Rs. 48/- also available in Hindi
101 Magic Tricks (In Colour) — 112 pp • Rs. 88/-
501 Astonishing Facts — 115 pp • Rs. 48/- also available in Hindi
501 Fascinating Facts — 104 pp • Rs. 48/- also available in Hindi, Bangla, Kannada & Assamese
Fun with Numbers — 115 pp • Rs. 48/- also available in Hindi
Incredible But True — 112 pp • Rs. 48/- also available in Hindi

How to solve Crossword Puzzles — 104 pp • Rs. 60/-
Magic for Fun — 112 pp • Rs. 48/- also available in Hindi, Kannada and Marathi
Magic for You — 124 pp • Rs. 40/- also available in Hindi
Magic for Children — 124 pp • Rs. 48/- also available in Hindi
Spicy Side of Speeches — 128 pp • Rs. 60/- also available in Hindi
The Funny side of English — 232 pp • Rs. 68/- also available in Hindi

Amusing Encounters of Daily Life — 124 pp • Rs. 68/-
Origin of 101 Everyday Things — 180 pp • Rs. 60/-
Strange But True Facts — 184 pp • Rs. 80/-
Monster — 104 pp • Rs. 68/-
The Witches of Wairiki — 176 pp • Rs. 68/-
The Woman in White — 144 pp • Rs. 80/-